Soviet and Post-Soviet Politics and Society (SPPS)

ISSN 1614-3515

Founded in 2004 and refereed since 2007, SPPS makes available affordable English-, German-, and Russian-language studies on the history of the countries of the former Soviet bloc from the late Tsarist period to today. It publishes between 5 and 20 volumes per year and focuses on issues in transitions to and from democracy such as economic crisis, identity formation, civil society development, and constitutional reform in CEE and the NIS. SPPS also aims to highlight so far understudied themes in East European studies such as right-wing radicalism, religious life, higher education, or human rights protection. The authors and titles of all previously published volumes are listed at the end of this book. For a full description of the series and reviews of its books, see www.ibidem-verlag.de/red/spps.

Editorial correspondence & manuscripts should be sent to: Dr. Andreas Umland, c/o DAAD, German Embassy, vul. Bohdana Khmelnitskoho 25, UA-01901 Kyiv, Ukraine. e-mail: umland@stanfordalumni.org

Business correspondence & review copy requests should be sent to: *ibidem* Press, Leuschnerstr. 40, 30457 Hannover, Germany; tel.: +49 511 2622200; fax: +49 511 2622201; spps@ibidem.eu.

Authors, reviewers, referees, and editors for (as well as all other persons sympathetic to) SPPS are invited to join its networks at www.facebook.com/group.php?gid=52638198614 www.linkedin.com/groups?about=&gid=103012 www.xing.com/net/spps-ibidem-verlag/

Recent Volumes

181   *Andrey Makarychev, Alexandra Yatsyk (eds.)*
Boris Nemtsov and Russian Politics
Power and Resistance
With a foreword by Zhanna Nemtsova
ISBN 978-3-8382-1122-0

182   *Sophie Falsini*
The Euromaidan's Effect on Civil Society
Why and How Ukrainian Social Capital Increased after the Revolution of Dignity
With a foreword by Susann Worschech
ISBN 978-3-8382-1131-2

183   *Andreas Umland (ed.)*
Ukraine's Decentralization
Challenges and Implications of the Local Governance Reform after the Euromaidan Revolution
ISBN 978-3-8382-1162-6

184   *Leonid Luks*
A Fateful Triangle
Essays on Contemporary Russian, German and Polish History
ISBN 978-3-8382-1143-5

185   *John B. Dunlop*
The February 2015 Assassination of Boris Nemtsov and the Flawed Trial of his Alleged Killers
An Exploration of Russia's "Crime of the 21st Century"
With a foreword by Vladimir Kara-Murza
ISBN 978-3-8382-1188-6

186   *Vasile Rotaru*
Russia, the EU, and the Eastern Partnership
Building Bridges or Digging Trenches?
ISBN 978-3-8382-1134-3

187   *Marina Lebedeva*
Russian Studies of International Relations
From the Soviet Past to the Post-Cold-War Present
With a foreword by Andrei P. Tsygankov
ISBN 978-3-8382-0851-0

188   *George Soroka,*
Tomasz Stepniewski (eds.)
Ukraine after Maidan
Revisiting Domestic and Regional Security
ISBN 978-3-8382-1075-9

189   *Petar Cholakov*
Ethnic Entrepreneurs Unmasked
Political Institutions and Ethnic Conflicts in Contemporary Bulgaria
ISBN 978-3-8382-1189-3

Vasile Rotaru

RUSSIA, THE EU, AND
THE EASTERN PARTNERSHIP

Building Bridges or Digging Trenches?

ibidem-Verlag
Stuttgart

Bibliographic information published by the Deutsche Nationalbibliothek
Die Deutsche Nationalbibliothek lists this publication in the Deutsche Nationalbibliografie;
detailed bibliographic data are available in the Internet at http://dnb.d-nb.de.

Bibliografische Information der Deutschen Nationalbibliothek
Die Deutsche Nationalbibliothek verzeichnet diese Publikation in der Deutschen
Nationalbibliografie; detaillierte bibliografische Daten sind im Internet über http://dnb.d-nb.de
abrufbar.

Cover picture: Eastern Partnership Summit in Riga 2015. © Secretariat of the Latvian Presidency of the
Council of the European Union, CC BY-SA 3.0 (s. https://creativecommons.org/licenses/by
sa/3.0/deed.en)

ISSN: 1614-3515

ISBN-13: 978-3-8382-1134-3

© *ibidem*-Verlag / *ibidem* Press
Stuttgart, Germany 2018

Contents

Part II
A Partnership for a Common Neighbourhood

Chapter 4
From the 'New Neighbourhood Initiative' to the Eastern
Partnership

Chapter 5
Russia's Contribution to the Inception of the EaP

Chapter 6
Russia's Relations with the EaP Countries after 2009

List of Acronyms

AA	Association Agreement
CIS	Commonwealth of Independent States
DCFTA	Deep and Comprehensive Free Trade Agreement
DPR	Donetsk People's Republic
EC	European Community
EEU	Eurasian Economic Union
ENP	European Neighbourhood Policy
EU	European Union
GU(U)AM	Georgia, Ukraine, (Uzbekistan), Azerbaijan, Moldova
LPR	Lugansk People's Republic
PCA	Partnership and Cooperation Agreement
USSR	Union of Soviet Socialist Republics

Foreword

Since the dissolution of the Soviet Union, EU-Russia relations have witnessed a sinusoidal evolution. The cycles of rapprochement (e.g. the beginning of the '90s, the Medvedev presidency) have been followed by periods of tension (e.g. the Primakov tenure as foreign minister, Putin's third presidential term). The mutual trust between the two actors has varied accordingly.

In the first years of post-Soviet Russia the relations with the EU/EC reached the highest level. Moscow had abandoned the bellicose rhetoric and was showing great willingness to integrate into the Western community, on the latter's conditions. From a rival and competitor Russia had become a listening pupil of the US and Western Europe. During the recent Ukrainian crisis, in contrast, Moscow's relations with Brussels deteriorated as had never happened before, during the post-Soviet period. Mutual accusations of violation of international law have been followed by mutual sanctions. The EU-Russia summits and the negotiations of the new Partnership and Cooperation Agreement have been suspended.

By and large, the disagreements over the past 25 years between the EU and Russia have been caused by three main elements: normative issues, energy relations and the shared neighbourhood—the latter being particularly present on Brussels-Moscow agenda after the launch of the Eastern Partnership (EaP) in 2009.

The former Soviet space is at the core of Russian foreign policy and the rapprochement of any other actor towards this region is regarded with high suspicion. Even the syntagm used for designation of the countries laying between Russia and the EU (Belarus, Moldova, Ukraine, Georgia, Armenia and Azerbaijan, which are included in the EaP) gave grounds for dispute. Brussels's proposed term 'common neighbourhood' was opposed by Moscow at first on the ground that it could have hinted some challenge to its sphere of influence, preferring instead the expressions 'countries adjacent to Russia' and 'countries adjacent to the EU' (Haukkala 2010: 137).

This way, it sought to specify the separate nature of the links that Russia and the EU have with their respective neighbourhoods.

In this book, we will use the syntagm 'common neighbourhood' for referring to six former Soviet countries: Armenia, Azerbaijan, Belarus, Georgia, Moldova and Ukraine, without implying any subjective position of either Russia or the EU. We will use as well the term 'near abroad' (ближнее зарубежье, [blizhneye zarubezhye]) as a synonym for the former Soviet space. We are aware that this syntagm was coined by the Russian foreign minister Andrey Kozyrev (1990–1996) in the early 1990s in order to denote a special *droit de regard* for Moscow in the former Soviet republics (Martinsen 2002: 2). By using it here, we do *not* suggest that the Kremlin has special rights in the former Soviet space. Rather we emphasise specifically Russian perspectives towards this area. As we focus only on six former Soviet republics, Armenia, Azerbaijan, Belarus, Georgia, Moldova and Ukraine, we will here *de facto* apply 'near abroad' only to this area.

This book comprises updated versions of the author's journal articles and some revised fragments from his previous books *The Eastern Partnership: A Turning Point in EU-Russia Relations?* (Military Publishing House, Bucharest, 2014) and *Between Integration and Intervention: Russia and the European 'Near Abroad' after 2009* (Military Publishing House, Bucharest, 2016). As the title suggests, the book analyses EU-Russia relations with a particular emphasis on the impact of the Eastern Partnership (EaP) on Moscow's relations with Brussels and the former Soviet space.

The book is divided into two main parts. The first part starts by assessing the differences between Moscow's and Brussels' worldviews, looks at the evolution of the Kremlin's foreign policy towards the EU since the dissolution of the Soviet Union until present; and delves into several events that had a particularly deep impact on EU-Russia relations, e.g. the Orange Revolution (2004); the 2008 Caucasus war; the Euromaidan (2013–2014); the annexation of Crimea (2014).

The second part of the book argues that the EaP represented a turning point in EU-Russia relations, determining Moscow to revise its attitude towards the Union. It also explains that, even if the EaP is a Brussels' initiative, it met the ambitions and aspirations of the six former Soviet republics that willingly joined the Partnership. We also argue that despite its opposition towards EU's initiative, Russia itself acted involuntarily as a propeller of the EaP. By aiming to keep the former Soviet republics close, Moscow often conducted an assertive/aggressive policy in the 'near abroad'. Such a strategy, however, had mostly opposite effects, causing Russia's neighbours to look elsewhere for guarantees of their sovereignty. Thus, from this perspective, the rapprochement of Moldova, Belarus, Ukraine and the three Caucasus republics with Brussels has not only been determined by EU's prosperity and soft power attractiveness, but also by the partner countries' existential needs.

The book seeks to serve a wide range of students and professors specialising on Russia, the EU and the former Soviet space in the fields of International Relations, Foreign Policy Analysis and Security Studies, as well as to think-tankers and policy makers.

Bucharest, April 2018

Part I
EU-Russia Relations:
From Cooperation to Distrust

Chapter 1
A Clash of Two Worldviews?

Introduction

The EU-Russian relationship has never been simple or smooth. The two partners often found their cooperation dominated by mutual distrust and divergent interests. Accusations of violations of democratic rules and values from one side and of using double standards from the other side have often poisoned the relationship between the two actors. The present chapter argues that the roots of disagreements between Russia and the EU should not be seen primarily in the Kremlin's leaders' authoritarianism and 'pragmatism' or the EU's insistence on norms and values, but rather in the more fundamental difference of the very nature of the two actors.

Locked in a realist worldview, based on concepts of balance of power and zero-sum games, Russia does not understand the win-win principle of the EU's political philosophy, fiercely opposing any sovereignty transfer and watching with scepticism the promotion of democratic rules and values beyond its neighbours' western borders. On the other side, the EU, a promoter of liberal institutionalism, finds Russia's policy to trend against the stream of the 21st century international system's order and sees the interdependence and sharing of common universal values as the key for stability and prosperity.

Neither Russia nor the EU has been content with this relationship. Despite economic interdependence, strategic partnership, official declarations of belonging culturally and historically to the same 'European family', or Russia's interest in participating in the integration process of the continent and creating a 'harmonious economic community stretching from Lisbon to Vladivostok' (Putin 2010), the two actors have found it difficult to agree on important issues, be it democratic values, the 'common neighbourhood', or energy relations. There has not been a single major treaty between

Russia and the EU that has not been preceded by difficult negotiations and infringements of the accepted terms during its implementation. Whether the Partnership and Cooperation Agreement, the Common Spaces or the commitments Russia made upon accession to the Council of Europe, the EU has frequently accused Moscow of not respecting, reinterpreting, or challenging the agreed rules. Furthermore, critique of Russia's growing authoritarianism, violation of free market principles, energy blackmail, or attempts at re-creating the Soviet empire is heavily present in Western analytical briefs and academic literature.

From Moscow's point of view, however, it is the EU that applies rules in a discretionary way, uses double standards, interferes in Russia's internal affairs and attempts to deprive Moscow of 'legitimate' spheres of influence for its own benefit. The Kremlin keeps emphasising that the West took advantage of its weakness in the 1990s and intends to do the same nowadays to the detriment of Russia's national interests. Hence, its scepticism towards Brussels's enhanced cooperation with the former Soviet republics and promotion of democratic values and standards beyond the EU's borders.

How should one interpret these contradictions between the EU and Russia? Is it a competition for influence, a confrontation between authoritarianism and democracy, a question of different values? According to Krastev (2008) the frictions between the two actors can be explained through the political clash between a modern state—Russia, and a post-modern entity—the EU. Starting from this point, we proceed further and will argue that the EU-Russian relationship is jeopardised by contradiction between two concepts underlying the two actors' worldviews: neorealism and liberal institutionalism.

1.   A realist power in a post-modern world

In a 2005 article, the Russian analyst, Dmitry Trenin summarised the essence of the current Russian worldview as such: 'the elites have left the 20th century behind—to go back to the 19th century' (Trenin 2005: 1). In other words, instead of adapting their policy to the post-Cold War international order, dominated by concepts of integration and globalisation, Russian political leaders reshaped their visions according to the pre-Cold War or even to the pre-World War I order, continuing to see the international arena through the lenses of *Realpolitik*. To better understand what Trenin's statement implies, we begin with a short assertion of the basic principles of (neo)realist theory.

From a (neo)realist perspective, the international system is anarchic, and comprises equally sovereign states that are the system's units. 'The equal of all the others, none is entitled to command, none is required to obey' (Waltz 1979: 88). There is no global government. The states act according to their own interests and they differ 'primarily by their greater or less capabilities for performing similar tasks' (Waltz 1979: 97). (Neo)realists assume that the main concern of the international system's units is security and survival. Therefore, states are rational actors that make strategic calculations. Facing the threat that other states may use force to harm or conquer them, the system's units are compelled to improve their relative power positions through arms build-ups, unilateral diplomacy and mercantile foreign economic policies (Karagiannis 2012: 2).

Realists understand international relations primarily as a struggle among the great powers for domination and stability: 'struggle for power … whenever [states] strive to realize their goal by means of international politics, they do so by striving for power' (Morgenthau 1965:27). National interest plays an important role within this context. For realists, it is the basic guide for responsible foreign policy (Jackson and Sørensen 2003: 87).

(Neo)realists argue also that great powers manage the international system so as to maintain international order. For classical realists, this is possible through the balance of power mechanism that prevents hegemonic world domination by any one great power, while for neorealists it is more likely to be achieved in a bipolar system than in a multipolar system. Mearsheimer (1993) claimed that the end of the Cold War bipolar order and the emergence of multipolar Europe would lead to instability, to the bad old ways of European anarchy and even to a renewed danger of international conflicts. With such assumptions, neorealists are arguably missing to properly account for an important post-Cold War process: the integration of European nation-states into the European Union — a new international relationship between the major and minor powers of Europe which the juxtaposition of bipolarism versus multipolarism does not fully reflect (Jackson and Sørensen 2003: 91).

Mearsheimer (1994/95) also argues that as long as the international system is anarchic, the system's actors are interested in maintaining their freedom of manoeuvre. Therefore, states are averse to any legally binding normative entanglements that would jeopardise their sovereignty and autonomy. Thus, for realists, institutions do not really make a difference, on the international level (Haukkala 2010: 25). Instead, they are the 'mere surface of reflections of underlying processes that involve the dynamics of power' and are important mainly for 'gauging the evolution of the structure of power in international society' (Young 1989: 60, 61). There should not be any international obligations in the moral sense of the word between independent states. The only fundamental responsibility of a system's unit should be to advance and defend its national interest.

Considering the above theoretical arguments and overviewing the last 25 years of Russian foreign policy, one can notice that, except for a short 'deflection' at the beginning of the 1990s, when — at least, on the surface — Moscow sought to integrate itself into the community of Western democracies and institutions, realism has characterised the Kremlin's post-Cold War foreign policy. What varied was the degree of persistence in following its goals. This variation was determined by the capabilities and resources Moscow had at its disposal, at a certain moment in time.

In fact, even the short period of international liberalism of 1992–1993 raises some questions. As Haukkala (2010: 173) argues, worldviews do not change quickly, and, therefore, it would be naïve to think that the Soviet worldview would have just disappeared along with the collapse of the Soviet Union. Suspicions concerning the honesty of Russian commitments to the values of international liberalism are also supported by Rumer's (2007: 14) assertion that Moscow, highly dependent on support from the US and Europe, did not have the luxury of pursuing a foreign policy in contradiction with the policy priorities of its principal donors, and had to make the impression of sharing the same political philosophy. This is confirmed also by the domestic events of 1993 and the foreign political patterns that followed it – i.e. an attempt to balance the competing goals of establishing diplomatic and security hegemony throughout the CIS area as well as regaining great power status in international councils, while at the same time cultivating its ties with the G7 states, collectively as well as individually. Thus, a more credible explanation seems to be that, during Kozyrev's tenure as Russian foreign minister, Moscow's policy was 'subordinated to the need to maintain at least appearance, if not the substance, of partnership with the West' (Lynch 2001:8, 15), while after the events of 1993, the Kremlin was unable any more to maintain the appearances of liberalism.

The appointment of Evgenii Primakov, a former deputy chairman of the KGB, as foreign minister, in January 1996, removed remaining appearances of liberalism in Russian foreign policy. The zero-sum pragmatism rooted in a highly traditional understanding of realism, characterised by anti-Westernism and the call for 'multipolarity' has marked the aftermath. With declarations like 'Russia has been and remains a great power, and its policy toward the outside world should correspond to that status', and 'Russia doesn't have permanent enemies, but it does have permanent interests', Primakov clearly promoted 'pragmatic nationalist' and 'Eurasianist' viewpoints (Donaldson and Nogee 2009: 116). However, the weak economy led to a 'fatalistic dualism' in Russia's foreign policy, a contradiction between aspiration and capacity, between what Moscow really wanted and what it was forced to do. Thus, Primakov's so-called pragmatism led to few positive results, alienating instead Russia's friends and confirming the hostility of those traditionally suspicious of its intentions (Sakwa 2008: 242).

Putin's era was marked by a new form of realism. With the advantage of Russia's economic recovery, the new leader combined Russia's traditional orientation of foreign policy towards *Realpolitik*. In other words, Vladimir Putin asserted Russia's national interest, seeking at the same time to integrate the country into the international community, but on its own terms. Stressing the fact that Russia is part of European civilization, the Kremlin insisted that Russia should be accepted as an equal of the international community and integrate itself, in its own way. This new realism did not imply that Russia abandoned its aspirations to global influence, to be a great power, but that it was pursuing a 'far more conscious attempt to match ambitions with resources' (Sakwa 2008: 242, 244–245).

Putin's realism distanced Russia from some elements of Primakov's traditional thinking and borrowed several features of Kozyrev's foreign policy vision. Russia is seen as an important pole, one of the handful of gravitational great powers that determine the shape and direction of the international system based on a balance of power. In order to be a voice heard and a presence to be reckoned with in world affairs, Putin sees integration into the international system as an important objective of Russian foreign policy. However, compared to Kozyrev's vision of an integration based essentially on common values, this time values and principles should play a minor role, if any at all. Considering the realist perspective of the international order determined by the balance of power and interests among countries, Russia should not indulge to be a passive member of the system but should participate in formulating the global agenda. Instead of accepting the guidance of other powers, which have their own selfish national interests, Russia should protect and follow its own goals by actively involving herself in world affairs (Rumer 2007: 23–24).

During Putin's second term, Russia's foreign policy became more assertive. Russia was not satisfied any more with mere recognition of its interests, it also demanded international prestige. Moscow insisted on its equal status with the US and EU in a multipolar world and wanted more weight in the resolution of global issues (Donaldson and Nogee 2009: 361). This assertive realism was maintained in the Medvedev doctrine and characterised Putin's third presidential term too.

A basic feature of Russian foreign policy is the 'supremacy' of the national interest that 'justifies the means'. It has remained the same since the fall of the Soviet Union. It refers to the need to ensure national security, promote economic prosperity of the country, and enhance international prestige — goals that have been pursued by Moscow regardless of who headed the ministry of foreign affairs or who was the tenant of the Kremlin. From the perspective of Russian leaders, security means first of all order, both on the domestic scene and in the border regions, as order leads to predictability and increased security, necessary for the prosperity of social, political and economic life. However, Moscow does not see order as a moral or normative issue, but as order for its own sake.

Domestically this trend is best expressed through the verticalisation of power as a 'need' for Russia's internal order; while external order is based on Russia's assumed 'great power role of security and welfare provider in the region as an inescapable task to itself and to the rest of the world' (Nygren 2008: 8). In as far as Russia perceives the former Soviet republics, the border regions, as important to its security and foreign goals, it seeks to 'keep order' around its periphery. Presuming that these states would end up in a security vacuum if left to their own devices (e.g. falling prey to general instability, aggravated by transnational crime, terrorism or inter-ethnic and inter-religious militancy), and thus bringing instability to Russia's doorstep (Rumer 2007: 25), Moscow tries to maintain its control over former possessions.

However, this does not only mean creating a security belt around Russia. Friendly, compliant governments of the former Soviet republics would contribute also to the economic security. Control over pipelines, key markets and labour migration play an important role for a Russia that is economically dependent on energy exports and with a continuous demographic decline since the collapse of the Soviet Union. Moreover, protecting this economic sphere of influence fits Russia's current mercantilist geopolitical frame of mind, offering the Kremlin important leverage vis-à-vis Europe (Rumer 2007: 27). By securing its position as the epicentre of power and influence in the neighbouring countries, Russia seeks to attain its highly sought after prestige and gain confirmation as a great power and as a pole in a multipolar world. As Trenin (2007: 81) argues, 'no great power ... walks alone'. Therefore, the former Soviet republics should play an important role in growing Russia's geopolitical strength. According to the realist worldview, a power, which is an important centre of gravity, will be a subject and not an object of international order. And as a subject of international order, Russia will take part in designing the international order and will be able to harmonise it with its own national interests (Chambers 2010: 124).

On the other side, becoming a strong gravitational pole fits Russia's strategy in international affairs, which it perceives in traditional balance-of-power terms, a concept that characterised international relations in the 19th and early 20th centuries. Within this context, Russia views itself as a pole in a multipolar world characterised by inter-power relations based on interests and where the order of the system can be maintained through a balance of the poles, so that none of them becomes too strong. In this 'game', shared values are at most of secondary importance—an approach that allows Russia to insist on respect for national sovereignty in neo-Westphalian terms and maintain its suspicion of transnational interaction (Romanova 2010: 75).

The concept of multipolarity also confers on Russia the lost status of a great power. As long as multipolarity implies a world of powers more or less equal at least in their right to shape the international order, if not in terms of inherent power capabilities (Mankoff 2009: 15), Moscow feels itself an equal of the US and prefers to deal with France, Germany, or Great Britain directly and not through the EU, favouring an international system where the large states are the main upholders of global order, and where smaller EU member states like Poland, Estonia, or Latvia 'do not have the right' to take part in the main decisions in world affairs, as they are condemned to gravitate around sovereign poles. According to this Russian perspective, only a great power can be truly sovereign (Krastev 2007) and able to pursue interest-based relations with other great powers of the system or balance them so that no pole becomes too strong.

In the spirit of multipolarity, Russia also seeks to strengthen those international institutions and laws that promote the sovereignty and equality of the world's major states, above all the UN Security Council and G8/G7, G20, i.e. great power clubs that do not limit its sovereignty in domestic affairs and impede the US to act without the support of other major powers (Mankoff 2009: 16). The Kremlin also rejects globalisation as an ideology of international hegemony of the dominant power system. Furthermore, as a 'real sovereign' Russia considers itself to have 'the capacity in reality (and not merely in declaratory fashion) to conduct independently its internal, external and defence policies, to conclude and tear up agreements, enter into strategic partnerships or not' (Kokoshin 2006: 63). Russia claims to have the ability and right to sustain an independent civilizational worldview (Sakwa 2011: 971) — a worldview based on concepts of multipolarity and balance of power.

Russia prefers to deal within the framework of bilateral relations even for transnational problems such as terrorism. The cooperation with the US after 9/11, for instance, had in the Kremlin's eyes the advantage of highlighting Russia's special relationship with the US concerning nuclear issues and terrorism, and to elevate thus its status above that of other powers. Furthermore, by adopting Washington's global war of terror as an organising principle for relations with the West, Russia attempted to reposition the relationship from integration to partnership — a partnership that would make the US acknowledge Russia as its equal. In addition, unlike multilateral pacts based on commitment to shared values, bilateral state-to-state relations avoid the creation of intrusive behavioural norms which could 'alter' a state's sovereignty (Mankoff 2009: 299, 15).

When dealing with the EU as a supranational structure, Russia addresses the relationship with the EU through the balance of power logic too. From Moscow's perspective, the Union is a potential pole and possibly an effective counterbalance to the US and NATO. In Putin's (2007a) words, Russia views

'European integration as an objective process which is a component part of a nascent multipolar world order. [I]t is important for us that the EU is increasingly becoming a more prestigious and influential centre of world politics, [and that] Russia intends to build its relations with the EU on the basis of a treaty and strategic partnership',

- and thus, on terms of equality. Therefore, it is not surprising that the strategic partnership with the EU is especially stressed when relations with the US are tense (Oldberg 2007: 20). Medvedev's proposal of a new European Security Treaty aiming to re-establish an indivisible security sphere reaching from Vancouver to Vladivostok also fits the context of balancing the US and NATO. The European Security Treaty would have inevitably undermined NATO and US influence in Europe.

Thus, Russian foreign policy has varied from a more accommodating realism of the early post-Soviet years, to traditional forms during Primakov's tenure, to a new realism during Putin's first term, and to a more assertive type after 2006. However, the substance of Russian policy remained the same. What differs is the degree of its assertiveness which is determined by national power. A good example in this respect is Medvedev's five-point foreign policy doctrine of 2008, which virtually reflects the same aspirations as the Foreign Policy Concept of 1993 (Sussex 2012: 208). This should not be surprising at all, if we take into consideration that the leading elites that shaped Russian foreign policy after 1992 grew up during the Cold War—many of them remaining in power for more than ten years, changing only in their public positions. Or, as one aide to President Medvedev observed 'when one resets a computer, one does not erase its memory' (Sussex 2012: 203).

2.   'A strange animal' or a state-of-the-art power?

Without its own army, but an economic power with its own currency and a rich market of over 500 million citizens, the EU plays an important role in the international arena. It is the largest supplier of development and technical assistance in the world, conducts peace-keeping missions of its member states to far-flung regions of the planet, leads in negotiations on climate change and on the establishment of the International Criminal Court (in opposition to the US), and seeks to expand its values, rules and norms in negotiations with third countries. The EU is, as Cameron (2007: 5) put it, 'a strange animal' — not quite a state but with more powers than many nation states in the actual international system.

Against the background of its supranational aspects, comparing it with a state can be inappropriate and limiting. Although a comparison with other international organisations seems to be thus more appropriate, that is, however, also limiting in as far as the EU's institutions and ambitions going well beyond the capacities and aims of most international organizations (Smith 2011: 160). With such characteristics, it is obvious that the EU is not and cannot be a traditional great power, and a realist 19th century system unit. Rather, it is a post-modern entity that still gives headaches as to how to be defined.

In the academic literature, the EU has been assessed in various ways: civilian normative, soft power imperialist, or neo-medieval power. However, as Youngs (2010: 3) argues, these are terms and metaphors do nothing but confirm that the EU is a uniquely international power and a 'particularly notable encapsulation of liberal values'; the EU is thus deemed to be 'a liberal superpower particularly well equipped for navigating a post-modern international system'. This statement is also supported by agreement among analysts that the EU has rejected realism and offers a different vision of international relations, compared with that pursued by the US. In particular, 'the EU has become the world's most effective and committed promoter of liberal political rights, collective security and multilateralism' (Youngs 2010: 3).

Within this context, Zimmerman's (2007) assessment of the EU as a realist power appears unjustified. Even if the foreign policy of the EU is made by its currently 28 members and although the member states might have realist sensibilities, this does not establish that the EU is a realist power. The Union is instead a liberal project, which is based on human rights, democracy and associated freedoms (Wood 2011: 245), and which tries to expand its principles and institutions in order to ensure cooperation between states and thus, the peace and stability of the international system — features that fit best the institutional liberal concept.

The liberal institutionalists accept the primacy of the state in the international system and that sovereignty is still sacrosanct. They, however, argue that institutions and economic interdependence prescribe states' 'behavioural roles, constrains [their] activity and shapes [their] expectations' (Keohane 1989:3) – as states seek to maximise their gains through cooperation. In support of the argument of stability and peace, the liberal institutionalists claim that there institutions made a significant difference in Europe after the end of the Cold War (Keohane and Hoffmann 1993), that they acted as 'buffers' to the shocks sent through Western Europe by the end of the Cold War and the reunification of Germany, hindering neorealist foresights of a return to instability in Western Europe, in a repetition of the first half of the 20th century.

Thus, from the institutional liberal perspective, a high level of institutionalisation significantly reduces the destabilising effects of multipolar anarchy. This is because international institutions promote cooperation between states, help reduce member states' fears of each other, and reduce the lack of trust between them (because information is available to all parties and the risk of cheating is reduced) – factors which are considered to be the main problems associated with international anarchy. Furthermore, international institutions provide a forum for negotiation between states. The EU has a number of such fora, starting with the Council of Ministers, the European Commission, and the European Parliament, that foster cooperation between states for their mutual advantages (Jackson and Sørensen 2003: 119-120).

Institutionalists do not deny the importance of material factors in the states' conduct of their foreign affairs. They instead highlight that the anarchy of the international system can be tempered by the need of states to cooperate. Interdependence and cooperation between states, based on commonly accepted norms and rules, contribute to the creation of 'a climate in which expectations of stable peace develop' (Nye 1993: 39). In other words, institutions can change state behaviour from one prone to war to another prone to peace and stability.

In addition, growing economic interdependence pushes states towards cooperation. A system's actor cannot act aggressively without risking economic penalties from other members of the international community. Furthermore, it becomes illogical for a state to threaten its commercial partners whose markets and investments are essential for the state's own economic development. Thus, to-day, when it became obvious that the 'trade state' rather than 'military state' is becoming dominant, and a state's welfare is determined by its participation in the international market of goods and services (Burchill 2008: 82), the EU – a power without any coercive force, but with the largest market in the world – gains considerable economic and commercial leverage towards third countries, making the promotion of universal norms and values beyond its borders easier and more effective.

Thus, the European common market became a considerable resource for exerting foreign normative influence. Various forms of interdependence between the EU and third countries, from association agreements and bilateral commercial agreements to encouragement to develop regional integration agreements on the model of Europe, allow the EU to transpose norms and values it considers of universal value. The Union does so by basing its relations with the rest of the world on the normative principles of peace, freedom and democracy, or, in the words of The Treaty on European Union (Art. 21), on

> 'the principles that have inspired its own creation, development and enlargement, and which it seeks to advance in the wider world: democracy, the rule of law, the universality and indivisibility of human rights and fundamental freedoms, respect for human dignity, the principles of equality and solidarity, and respect for the principles of the United Nations Charter and international law'.

The EU's preference for norms and values reminds of Kant's 'Perpetual Peace' – where the cosmopolitan order requires two essential elements: the pacific nature of the republics and the civilising power of trade (Laidi 2008: 10). Kant gave priority to values over territoriality – and so does the EU. The two elements were taken up almost word for word in the Solana 2003 report, intended to set out Europe's strategic doctrine following the US invasion of Iraq: 'the quality of international society depends on the quality of governments: the best protection for our security is a world of well-governed democratic states', and 'trade and developing policies can be powerful tools for promoting reforms' (Solana J. 2003).

This statement fits the liberal internationalist inside-out view of the changed international system: the endogenous determines the exogenous. In other words, as more states implement liberal values internally, the risks of conflicts between states diminish; as democracy spreads, so does international peace. It is less likely that democratic states will resort to military actions in order to solve their disagreements. With political elites accountable to their citizens, democratic governments will not jeopardise the security and well-being of their electors or risk international sanctions. At the same time, free trade breeds mutually constraining interdependence between the international system's actors and assists the development of poorer countries (Youngs 2010: 2).

The majority of analysts agree that the EU's greatest achievement has been to end the *Realpolitik* order that dominated Europe for almost four centuries. Former German Foreign Minister, Joschka Fischer, described the EU as a regional political system based 'on the rejection of the European balance-of-power principle and the hegemonic ambitions of individual states that had emerged following the Peace of Westphalia in 1648' (Hill and Smith 2005: 368). The EU has proven that cooperation between states is possible and demonstrates that realists are wrong when they insist that anarchy condemns states to compete for military power and to become involved in major wars. Institutionalists do not deny the anarchic character of the international system. However, they argue that, through institutional cooperation and finding common interests, inter-state harmony is possible. Within this context, trade and economic relations can be important elements for ensuring peace and stability. The very inception of the EU was based on these elements and ended the historical antagonism between France and Germany.

After the end of the Cold War, the EU added to its earlier project of eliminating war between European powers the new challenge of encouraging democratic politics and respect for human rights across the continent (Hill and Smith 2005: 368). The enlargement has been the most effective instrument in this respect. Accepting and implementing the *acquis communautaire*, the candidate states made the extension of EU norms, rules and constraints to the eastern part of continent possible, making instability and conflict in the wider post-communist region less likely (Cameron 2007: 62). Even when accession is not offered, the EU tries to bring its neighbours as close as possible to its community of values through its power of attraction and various contractual arrangements. An example in this respect is the Eastern Partnership with the six former Soviet countries that lie between the EU and Russia.

3.   An inevitable clash?

Whereas the EU was born from the need to avoid the dangers of nationalism and to stop the rivalries of European nation-states in the first half of the 20th century, the Russian Federation emerged in the context of the failure of post-national politics and the disintegration of the Soviet Union. Both actors have been marked by past developments: the EU by the experience of the 1930s, Russia by the troubles of the 1990s (Krastev 2007). These negative experiences are having a great impact on their political structures and worldviews.

In international relations theory, different worldviews lead actors to perceive the world and issues at stake differently. Hence the differences in understanding the norms and rules that pertain to the scope, the nature of objects of contention, the relationship with sovereignty, and the logic of interaction in a given international institution (Haukkala 2010: 3). This premise leads us to assert that the misunderstanding between Russia and the EU should not be sought in their rival interests or unshared values, but in their political incompatibility.

As Krastev (2007) argues, the confrontational situation between the EU and Russia should not be perceived as a clash between democracy and authoritarianism, as history has shown that democratic and authoritarian states are able easily to cooperate; but as a clash between a post-modern actor — the EU, and a traditional modern one — Russia. The different logic of worldviews of post-modern and modern actors leads to political incompatibilities, which, in turn, generate frictions and misunderstandings. The differences in how the EU and Russia see themselves and the world, their specificity as well as insufficient equality and equivalence make both actors understand reciprocity differently while insisting that they speak about the same thing (Romanova 2010).

Thus, while for the EU reciprocity in relation with Russia means to share the same values, norms and standards, and an agenda for a transformation of Russia towards the 'European' model, Moscow has a more traditional sovereign understanding of the relationship with the EU. For Russia, political equality and preservation of its sovereignty should underlie proper reciprocity. Moscow agrees on the importance of normative convergence. However, it does not accept it extensively, but as a much more selective process which can advance only in so far as it benefits Russian political and economic interests (Haukkala 2010: 170), and thus excludes the EU from having any influence in its domestic spheres.

In this context, the normative approach favoured by the EU becomes a major source of conflict in the relationship with Russia. Brussels sees the 'Europeanisation' of Russia through the lenses of a liberal win-win situation that aims at the international stability and prosperity of both actors, and argues that the EU's rules and standards are not only the EU's normative baggage, but are shaped according to universal democratic principles. Russia, in contrast, perceives the EU's value-based approach as an attempt to meddle in its internal affairs, as an attempt to enforce its own legislation as a condition for cooperation (Kulhanek 2010: 56). Furthermore, as many political elites in Russia consider that, in the 1990s, the West took advantage of the weakness of their country and ruthlessly exploited Moscow's complacent attitude, there is a widespread opinion that any concession now would be interpreted by the West as capitulation (Sakwa 2008: 250).

Thus, Surkov's concept of 'sovereign democracy' could not fit Russia's notions of independence and great power status better. A mixture of the anti-populism of the 19th century French political thinker François Guizot and of the anti-pluralism as well as decisionism of the German political philosopher Carl Schmitt (Krastev 2007), sovereign democracy is based on the idea that the state should set the rhythm of economic and political changes without any interference from abroad. As the Kremlin ideologist defined it, a truly sovereign democracy is one whose goals and methods, both at home and abroad, should be made solely on the basis of calculations of national interest and not under any pressure to conform to behavioural norms (Mankoff 2009: 15–16). For the Kremlin, sovereignty is a matter of capacity. It implies economic independence, solid strategic and cultural identity, military strength and tends to lose its representative dimension, justifying instead the development and build-up of power (Parmentier 2008: 109). The emphasis on sovereignty is present not only in the domestic sphere, but also in Russian foreign policy, which appears to make the Kremlin less and less interested in coordinating its foreign policies with those of the West (Mankoff 2009: 15–16).

However, the concept of sovereign democracy comes into direct opposition with the very philosophy of the EU. As a supranational entity, the EU sees mutual interference in each other's domestic affairs and security based on openness and transparency as key elements of the post-Cold War European order. Compared with the Russian approach, the EU emphasizes far less sovereignty or the separation of foreign from domestic affairs, promoting instead a deliberate increase in mutual dependence and vulnerabilities between European states and rejecting the use of force as a means for settling conflicts (Krastev 2007). The Kremlin, on the other side, understands international relations in terms of the Westphalian concept of nation-states, where sovereignty is constituted by territoriality and the exclusion of foreign actors from domestic governance (Kulhanek 2010: 61). In other words, while the EU understands sovereignty as 'a seat at a table', Russia perceives the concept as the right of government to do what it wants within its territory and to eliminate its enemies abroad, even in the centre of London (Krastev 2007).

Russian political leaders are thus locked into a zero-sum mentality, incapable of understanding the win-win culture that underlies the European integration process. The Kremlin does not accept the idea of defining a political relationship in terms of 'sovereignty bargains': gaining disproportionally shared benefits in return for giving up some autonomy — the kind of bargains that are defended by the European Commission (Techau 2012) and that have proved to be a successful recipe for peace and prosperity in Europe.

Moreover, the EU leaders talk about partners rather than allies — even if they talk about 'friends', and they rarely use the word 'enemies', but rather speak of non-cooperative states (Portela 2007). In contrast, Russian political leaders still see the world through a Schmittian interpretation of politics. According to Carl Schmitt:

'the specific political distinction to which political actions and motives can be reduced is that between friend and enemy.... A world in which the possibility of war is utterly eliminated, a completely pacified globe, would be a world without the distinction between friend and enemy and hence a world without politics' (Schmitt 1996: 26, 35).

This is a philosophy in direct contradiction with the EU's vision of the world.

On the other side, while Russia vehemently opposes any interference in its domestic affairs, it sees nothing wrong with meddling in the affairs of others. Its policy in the former Soviet republics places Russia in, what Stephen Krasner referred to, as the 'organised hypocrisy' of sovereignty (Sussex 2012: 208–209). For Moscow, these states are its sphere of influence; they are doomed to gravitate around it — the sovereign pole of power, as from Moscow's perspective, only great power can be truly sovereign (Krastev 2007). This approach contradicts EU foreign policy based on cooperation, sharing interests and goals, voluntary integration into the European values community and the spread of Western ideals and institutions to its neighbours as a natural step in the progression of liberalism and democracy.

Thus, despite a common neighbourhood, the EU and Russia understand differently the evolutions in that region. While Russia sees geopolitics around every corner (Mankoff 2009: 281), basing its foreign policy on European practices and ideologies of the 19th century, the EU is promoting a post-modern order based on 21st century realities. The defence of territory from enemies is at the core of Schmitt's theory according to which the political order is first of all a spatial order before being a normative one. He does not deny the relevance of norms, yet subordinates them to the defence of territoriality. In other words, Schmitt favours *topia*, the taking of the land, to *utopia* (Laidi 2008: 9). The same philosophy underlies Russian foreign and security policy, which explains the importance given to hard power and the wrong understanding of soft power. From this point of view the confrontation between Russia and the EU is one between a Kantian (Europe) and a Schmittian (Russia) power.

Russia's special interest in the former Soviet republics is also directly linked to its foreign policy doctrine being based on a balance of power approach. Moscow perceives the maintenance of its influence in the 'near abroad' both as a necessary condition for its security (i.e. the shielding of its borders from destabilising Western democracy promotion that led to revolutions in Ukraine and Georgia and preventing these countries from joining NATO), and as necessary for enhancing its prestige vis-à-vis the other poles of the multipolar international system.

However, Russia's insistence and promotion of the concept of balance of power and its mercantilist geopolitical approach are undermining the philosophy of the EU, stimulating the renationalisation of the foreign policy of its member states (Krastev 2008). Worse, Moscow's insistence on a balance of power as the foundation of a new European order threatens the very existence of the EU. It would only restore the 19th century and early 20th century European rivalry, making cohabitation of member states within the EU impossible. This prospect, in turn, fits the Kremlin's 'prophesy' that the EU is a temporary phenomenon with no future (Krastev 2007). Its balance of power approach prescribes: as long as it still represents a pole of the multipolar world, Russia should seek to weaken the EU in order to grow its own power and prestige on the international arena.

For Russia, the preference for bilateral relations with the EU's member states serves not only its nation-state-centric view of the international system but also its authoritarian internal order. Dealing with individual states, Moscow expects that criticism of its domestic affairs are avoided. Its 'sovereign democracy' project should preserve it from EU 'threats', i.e. of the Union's insisting on human rights and openness. By marginalising the EU's policy of democracy promotion, the current political leaders secure their own chairs. Such an approach is also necessary to prevent the potential nightmare of ethnic and religious-based politics that could arise from territorial disintegration of the Russian Federation (Krastev 2007).

Hence, the EU's refusal to separate the promotion of democracy and harmonisation of values, rules and norms from 'pragmatic' economic relations is considered by many Russian analysts to be the main cause of misunderstandings between the EU and Russia. However, even hypothetically admitting that this separation could happen, there would still be weighty conceptual differences that would hinder close EU-Russian relations. Wallander (2005) argues that Russia does not have a foreign policy driven by economic growth for economic growth's sake. Instead, its foreign policy is driven by economic growth for the sake of political autonomy and global positioning. Within this context, state intervention in all spheres of the economy is seen as necessary for avoiding the 'selling' of the national economy to foreigners and to ensure that profits will be used according to the state's and not individuals' interests. The de-privatisation of some sectors (oil and natural gas, banking, the automobile industry, etc.) and the growing assertiveness of the public authorities support the idea that the state is the key driver, the subject of modernisation (Romanova 2010: 76).

Russia's state controlled economic vision comes into direct opposition with the EU's market- and rule-based economic approach. These characteristics, as Sutela (2007) argues, demonstrate that the EU and Russian approaches to reciprocity reflect differences between 'liberal and authoritarian capitalisms'. For the EU, it is primarily a matter of commonly agreed access to markets and investments. In other words, after the rules have been established: let the best competitor win. The EU tries to guarantee economic players equality of opportunities, limiting public authorities' interference and letting private actors take a lead. For Russia, it is primarily a matter of asset swaps assumed to be of similar values (Sutela 2007).

In addition to the differences already mentioned, Bova (2010) provides a cultural perspective of incompatibilities between the EU and Russia. Appealing to David Gress's book *From Plato to NATO* and Samuel Huntington's *The Clash of Civilizations*, he explains the cultural differences between the two actors which shape the way

how they see and interpret the world. Bova's conclusions – the an-
tithesis of the Western and Russian political cultural characteristics,
are summarized in the chart below:

**Table 1:   Political cultural differences between Russia and
the West**

Essential values and orientations	
Western political culture	**Russian political culture**
- Separation of church and state: the idea of two separate spheres of influence, one spiritual and one secular	- Unity of church and state: a symbiotic relationship between the Orthodox Church and Russian state
- Rule of law: governance happens via rules to which all citizens, including leaders, are subject	- Personalised authority: 'a succession of strong, autocratic monarchs' and 'attachment to political authority'
- Social pluralism: diverse groups, classes and interests exist and are accepted as legitimate	- *Sobornost'* (togetherness): implies a collective will of the people and its organic unity for a common purpose
- Representative bodies: the parliament and other institutions are the basis of modern democracy and represent the interests of diverse groups	- Statism: Putin in his 1999 Millennium Manifesto: 'Our state and its institutions and structures have always played an exceptionally important role in the life of the country and its people...'
- Individualism: a commitment to individual rights and liberties are at the basis of the concept of human rights	- Order: continued emphasis on order is so prevalent that it can come at the expense of freedom and liberty

This juxtaposition may appear oversimplified and exaggerated or
as containing inaccurate cultural stereotypes. Nevertheless, references to these characteristics are commonplace among observers
both inside and outside Russia (Bova 2010: 24–25). As long as politics comprises people who see the world through stereotypes, the
elements mentioned in the chart can give us some clues about the
way the Russian worldview is shaped.

Conclusions

Russia continues to look different from its major Western neighbour in some fundamental aspects. While the EU advocates postnational politics in a new post-Cold war era, Russia tries to build its statehood and shape its foreign policy according to European practices and ideologies of the 19th century. For Moscow, the European order should be a mixture of a 'concert of Europe' and a policy of combining an opening to the West with a rejection of any Western interference in domestic politics (Krastev 2007)—an idea reminiscent present-day China's approach to international relations, as well as a return, in some ways, to pre-Cold War practices.

The source of the current confrontation between the EU and Russia is thus a clash of two antagonistic worldviews: a modern approach to international relations, in the sense of the *Realpolitik* followed by the Kremlin; and a post-modern approach to foreign policy embodied in the supranational structures of the EU. The gap between the political cultures of Russia and the West is thus still big. If we take into consideration that the transition from monarchy to democracy took centuries in Western Europe, we should not reasonably expect a country that has never experienced real democracy to make the transition from communism to democracy in only two decades. Haukkala (2010: 173) correctly argues that worldviews do not change overnight. Current Russian political leaders were educated during Soviet times and it would be naïve to think that their view of the world would have changed radically with the disappearance of the Soviet Union.

Chapter 2
EU-Russia Relations between the Cold War and Georgian War

Introduction

Being officially 'strategic partners', yet having different geopolitical approaches, the EU and Russia often find their cooperation dominated by mutual distrust and divergent interests. As argued in the previous chapter, while Moscow continues to think in terms of traditional international relations, Brussels rejects the notion of spheres of influence and is instead guided by the concepts as normative power and Europeanisation. Put simply, while Russian policy is based on interests, the EU's is based on values (Nygren 2009: 132).

These differences have led many scholars to question whether the Russian Federation and the European Union can be actually considered strategic partners. In order to make a strategic partnership work, mutual trust is necessary. The Kremlin's policies in the energy field, non-observance of voluntarily adopted commitments to democratic values and human rights, or 'Potemkin democracy' presented as real political pluralism all undermine EU confidence in Russia. However, as Wiegand argues, size, proximity, history, economic interdependence and a simple comparison with some of the EU's other 'strategic partners' contradict the sceptical scholars (Wiegand 2008: 14).

When analysing EU-Russia relations, the direct link between the internal evolution of Russia and its foreign affairs is striking. The strengthening of the 'power vertical', the re-centralisation of the 'Federation', and the introduction of the concept of 'sovereign democracy', have all left their mark on Russian foreign policy. These trends have translated into search for an increase in international prestige, removal of Western leverage and restriction of the impact of international law and world public opinion on Russia's domestic policies (Oliker, Crane, Schwartz and Yusupov 2009: 89).

Add to these elements the larger international contexts of the EU-USA relationship and Russia-NATO relations, and we have a complete picture of EU-Russia relations — with lengthy negotiations between the two partners, friction in areas where Russia possesses advantages, and difficulties in developing an institutionalised relationship.

1. EU-Russia relations during the Yeltsin presidency

After the collapse of the Soviet Union, Russia was perceived by the West as a *tabula rasa*, upon which new liberal ideas could be made to stick with ease (Haukkala 2010: 173). Under the impact of Fukuyama's *End of History* euphoria, the West believed that democracy would fill the gap left by the defeated communist ideology. The beginning of the 1990s was seen as a 'formative moment' for Russia. Europe was ready to help the country to enter the 'community of civilised states' and believed that it could work with the new Russia to mutual benefit.

The most popular words in Russia at that time were democratisation and privatisation. The Kremlin leader kept saying that Russia was a European country and wanted to be recognised as a European partner. Yeltsin and his foreign minister Kozyrev established two main goals of Russian foreign policy: to become full members of the 'community of civilised states' and to attract as much external support as possible for social, economic and political reform attempts (Kozyrev 1992). It seemed that Yeltsin and his entourage were 'anti-communist, pro-market, pro-West, pro-democracy' and sought to dismember, what Ronald Reagan called, the 'evil empire' (Haukkala 2010: 71). The Westernisers were dominating Russian domestic and foreign policy thinking.[1] The European

---

1   According to Tsygankov (2006), over history, Russia has developed three schools of foreign policy thinking: Westernist, Statist and Civilisationist. Westernisers emphasise Russia's similarity with the West which they see as the most viable and progressive civilisation in the world. Statists put emphasis on the state's ability to govern and maintain political and social order. They emphasise the values of power, stability and sovereignty before the values of freedom and democracy. Civilisationists have always seen Russian values as different from those of the West and have even attempted to spread Russian values abroad.

Community was hoping and expecting that the post-communist 'honeymoon' would continue and Russia would join the democratic community.

However, these hopes did not last long. Already by 1993, the democratisation euphoria was fading and the Kremlin was returning to a more traditional foreign policy. This fact was motivated not only by the disappointment about the absence of a miraculous rate of economic growth, which should have offered Russians the same standard of living as in Western Europe, and the frustration about the defeat in the Cold War. Moreover, various Soviet structures were not completely demolished in 1991–1992.

It would, in any way, have been naïve to think that the Soviet worldview would have just disappeared overnight along with the formal state structures of the Soviet Union, thus enabling a 'thoroughly unencumbered' search for a new worldview (Haukkala 2010: 173). With former members of the Communist Party still in leading positions, claiming now to be democrats, there was no clear break with the past as had happened in the other former Warsaw Pact members. Furthermore, the end of the Cold War seems to have failed to remove some old antagonisms (Andréani 2008: 31). The political crisis of 1993, which brought Russia to the verge of civil war, made it clear that the country was not going to share the same values as the just created European Union. Thus, the beginning of the 1990s should be better seen, as Haukkala argues, as a 'period of complete intellectual and ideological confusion in the ruling circle of Russia', which resulted in a 'brief and haphazard emulation of Western/European ideas and ideals, followed by a growing rejection of them' (Haukkala 2010: 173) — rather than an honest propensity to democratise the country.

After the dismissal of the Soviet Union, the West was worried about the domestic situation in Russia. There was concern that, because of its weakness, Russia would not be able to deal with proliferation of nuclear missiles and the spread of terrorism. The general opinion was that a stronger Russia could cope more easily with

---

They have sought to challenge the Western system of values insisting on Russian cultural superiority.

these problems. Within this context, at the beginning of January 1992 the foreign ministers of the European Community (EC) met in Brussels to discuss the situation of the former USSR. It was decided that negotiations for cooperation agreements would start with four former Soviet republics: Russia, Belarus, Ukraine and Kazakhstan. Given its importance, Russia was the first country with which the Commission initiated the discussions. After his visit to Moscow in March 1992, the Commissioner for External Relations, Frans Andriessen suggested a new series of commercial and cooperation agreements with Russia and the other three former Soviet republics. The initiative was driven by the demand of the Russian foreign minister Kozyrev for a new commercial agreement during his visit in Brussels two months later: the Russian official asked for hurried negotiations as the EC-USSR Trade and Cooperation Agreement was outdated.

The negotiations for the Partnership and Cooperation Agreement (PCA) started in November 1992. It was expected that the process would be short. However, the negotiations took almost two years. There were two main issues which delayed the conclusion of the agreement: Russia was pushing for more trade concessions and a more generous long-term perspective in the form of a free trade area than was envisaged in the agreement draft, and the EC was insisting on applying political conditionality which was a source of concern on Russia's part (Haukkala 2010: 76).

It was clear that it was Russia that needed the EU more and not vice versa. Economic aid and access to the European market being imperative for a Russia plagued by a severe crisis. However, despite this strong asymmetry, the Kremlin succeeded in getting enough concessions from the EC/EU. Europe was afraid of not 'losing' Russia and was convinced that it had to support it in order not to deviate from the stated objective of being part of the democratic community and agreed to make concessions even though they initially had been seen as unacceptable.

The most obvious example in this context is the revitalisation of the negotiations in the aftermath of the political crisis in Russia in October 1993. The EU believed that it would be better to anchor Russia in an institutional frame so that the economic and political changes became irreversible, the cost of signing PCA being less than not signing it and 'losing' Russia. Thus, it was not Russia's power but its weakness that resulted in a series of important break-throughs in the process of negotiations (Haukkala 2010: 76). The 'weakness power', defined by Haukkala as the ability to extract concessions from other powers precisely because of your weakness and the 'potentially disastrous instability that continuation of that weakness might bring' (Haukkala 2010: 47), characterised the entire period of the Yeltsin government's relations with the EC/EU, particularly at the beginning of the 1990s.

The Partnership and Cooperation Agreement (PCA) was finally concluded in June 1994, during the Corfu summit. At the end of the signing ceremony, Yeltsin declared that now the hard part would start with the implementation of the agreement. Nevertheless, he assured the European partners that 'Russia will be an honest, loyal and trustful partner' (European Report 1994).

The PCA is primarily an economic agreement. However, the respect for democracy, the principles of international law and human rights play an important role too. A Common Declaration annexed to the PCA states clearly that 'the respect for the human rights represents an essential element of the agreement'. One can assume that if there is any proof of serious violations of human rights or of democratic values in Russia, the EU could suspend the PCA (Webber 2000: 74). The 'weakness power', however, seems to have prevented this from happening as the further evolution of EU-Russia relations showed.

After less than half a year since the Corfu summit, Russia proved one more time that it was going to be a difficult partner. The indiscriminate and disproportionate use of force and the flagrant violations of human rights during the first Chechen War, from December 1994 to August 1996, raised new doubts about Russia's commitment to European common values. Consequently, the EU delayed the ratification of the PCA and was seeking new solutions to keep its partner anchored in the democratic community. The Chechen war highlighted the need for a more definite approach towards Russia. The EU had to face a new reality.

In 1995, the Commission adopted the first EU Strategy on Russia. The document stated that the aim of the partnership with Russia was

'to promote the democratic and economic reform process, to enhance respect for human rights, to consolidate peace, stability and security in order to avoid new dividing lines in Europe and to achieve the full integration of Russia into the community of free and democratic nations'.

The strategy established the mechanisms and principles through which the integration would take place (Haukkala 2010: 95). The EU was again ready to help Russia — even if it had to turn a blind eye to serious violations of human rights.

The need to 'lock Russia into an institutional arrangement' in order to prevent 'the rollback of Russian democracy and economic reforms in the country' (Haukkala 2010: 89) also seems to have stood behind the acceptance of the country to the Council of Europe in 1996. In fact, the decision was taken without Russia meeting all the criteria (Malfliet and Partmentier 2010: 1). Council and Union hoped that the new status would enable Russia to 'learn democracy'.

The Council of Europe was the first Western European institution to have been created after the Second World War in order to protect human rights, democracy and the rule of law. This 'club of democratic European countries', designed initially as an association against the communist bloc, became, at the beginning of 1990s, a 'school of democracy' for the former members of Warsaw Pact. Before becoming members of the Council, these countries had to sign the European Convention of Human Rights and its most important additional protocols. By signing and ratifying those documents, the former communist countries became bound to honour the obligations that they had taken on by their own free will (Malfliet and Partmentier 2010: 8). That is why the acceptance of Russia as a member of the Council of Europe was seen as of crucial importance (Malfliet and Partmentier 2010: 8), and it was expected that Russia would follow the same path as the other former members of Warsaw Pact. However, these hopes were soon shattered.

Instead of 'learning democracy', Russia started challenging European values, and trying to establish new rules.

As the representation in the Council of Europe depends on the population and income of its constituent members, Russia made it very clear that it could take advantage of its position: Russia received 18 seats in the Parliamentary Assembly in Strasbourg, becoming with France, Germany, Italy and Great Britain, one of the five largest national delegations. In August 1996, Viktor Chernomyrdin, when approved for a second term as prime minister, declared that 'Russia was and will remain a great power' and, by definition, a great power does not take orders from anyone (Trenin 2011: 207).

Thus, as a member of the Council of Europe, Russia began to question the universality of European democratic values. The Kremlin started accusing Europe of using 'double standards' in the area of human rights, claiming that while the West was criticising Russia for not complying with common values, Baltic states were tolerated for violating the rights of ethnic Russians. The challenge to European values would become more obvious during Putin's presidency when, against European standards and norms, the Kremlin would assert its own concept of democracy and human rights – the already mentioned notion of 'sovereign democracy' (Malfliet and Partmentier 2010: 11).

In 1997, the PCA was ratified. However, the first Chechen War showed the EU that the agreement was not enough for a constructive relationship with Moscow. In addition, the severe economic and financial crisis in Russia, in August 1998, and the problems in the implementation of the PCA made EU-Russia relations more complicated. Within this context, it was again the 'weakness power' that made the EU adopt, in 1999, its Common Strategy on Russia (Haukkala 2010: 93).

The aim of the new strategy was to promote a stable, open, democratic Russia, governed by the rule of law and with a prosperous market economy. This development would help the EU and Russia to live 'in harmony together', as Javier Solana, the High Representative for the Common Foreign and Security Policy, declared (Pinder and Shishkov 2002: 113). At the beginning of the document it is stated that, 'a firmly anchored [Russia] in a united Europe free of new dividing lines, is essential to lasting peace on the continent'. The Strategy supported 'the integration of Russia into a wider area of cooperation in Europe' (Common Strategy of the European Union on Russia 1999). The document was conceived for a period of four years.

Moscow did not welcome with open arms the adoption of the EU's strategy, being irritated by the fact that Europe 'considered Russia more as an object of foreign policy of the united Europe, rather than an equal partner' (Haukkala 2010: 100). Accordingly, four months after the EU's Common Strategy came a Russian response called *The Medium-Term Strategy for Development of Relations between the Russian Federation and the European Union (2000–2010)* – a 'demanding and irritable response', as a British analyst concluded (Haukkala 2010: 100). The Russian strategy covered a similar agenda as that of the EU. It reiterated Moscow's support for a strengthened partnership with the European Union and highlighted the interest in a multipolar world, with 'an emphasis on international law and the disuse of force' (*Strategiya razvitiya otnoshenii Rossiiskoi Federatsii s Evropeiskim Soyuzom na srednesrochnouyu perspektivu* 2000), so that any single state could not impose its will through force, as Moscow argued the United States had done in Kosovo (Mankoff 2009: 153). The document was elaborated under the new Prime Minister, Vladimir Putin, and was soon complemented by the adoption of the National Security Concept, in January 2000, and the Foreign Policy Concept, in June 2000. A new phase in Russian foreign policy was starting.

2.   Vladimir Putin and 'Great Russia'

Leadership plays a very important role in Russia. It is even often argued that the country has a cultural predisposition for highly-personalised leadership, especially in times of turmoil. Becoming President after a period of chaos and despair, as well as being young, dynamic and determined to restore order, Putin quickly won the confidence of most Russians. The population wanted a strong ruler to 'save' the country and to restore its greatness. This situation has only smoothed the new leader's method of strengthening the power of his office.

Shortly after Putin was appointed President of the Russian Federation, on December 31, 1999, he started—what may be called—a 'Thermidor', a classic counter-act, announcing the return of the State. In a search for order and stability, Putin devoted himself to rebuilding the state and regaining territory from business elites, civil society, media and the West (Medvedev 2008: 225). Soon Russian domestic and foreign policy became more 'presidential' and personal. Within this context, elements of Putin's biography may be relevant to understanding Russian foreign affairs between 2000–2008. The President's past as a former KGB agent, his propensity for doing things in secret, the often excessive suspicion, and rejection of all that is foreign or hard to understand left their mark on Russian foreign policy (Nygren 2008: 6).

The 'Russia at the Turn of the Millennium' Manifesto, published on the pages of *Nezavisimaya gazeta* in December 1999, while Putin was still serving as Prime Minister, announced the new direction of Russia's foreign policy. The ideas of this article would be found afterwards in the Foreign Policy Concept, adopted in June 2000. Putin pleaded for a stronger state by 'combining the universal principles of a market economy and democracy with Russian realities', highlighting that 'Russia was and will remain a great power' (Putin 1999).

Vladimir Putin was supported by a large majority of Russians, frustrated by economic dislocations, and Moscow's 'defeat' in the Cold War. At the popular level, good relations with the West should have brought economic advantages and a rise in the standard of living. As time passed, however, it became clear that these would not happen as fast as anticipated. Externally, Russia's sensitivity towards NATO's expansion and especially the NATO intervention in Serbia disappointed the Westernisers and confirmed the suspicions of the Statists, who believed that the West wanted to gain maximum benefit from its strong position after the Cold War and Russia's weakness. The Kremlin had hoped that, as the Cold War had ended, Europe would develop a new security strategy based on such institutions as OSCE. But the West preferred to expand NATO, violating a promise allegedly given to Soviet leaders by US Secretary of State James Baker that, in exchange for a united Germany being in NATO, the expansion of that body would not proceed an inch farther eastward (Brown 2009: 51).

Facing a disastrous balance of Yeltsin's governance, Putin felt obliged to distance himself from the policies of his predecessor. Security policy was revised, and the notion of 'foreign strategic threats' to national security reappeared as well as the term 'potential enemy', both being associated with NATO (Grachev 2005: 256). Putin highlighted the importance of relations with the EU, taking advantage of every opportunity to declare that Russia considers itself part of Europe and seeks to participate in the integration process of the continent (Lo 2003: 102). The Russian leadership wanted to see the country again as a great power, but was aware that this was not possible without a strong economy. Within this context, the new foreign policy was directed towards a transition from the Soviet model of diplomacy, obsessed by security and centred on the military balance model, and towards a strategy based on the development of the economy (Grachev 2005: 259), within which the European market played an important role.

However, there was a paradox: Russia had the ambition to be recognised again as a great power, but was driven by its fear of isolation, especially from Europe. The EU, in general, exerts a strong magnetic force upon the states surrounding it, as trade and geographic proximity make it an evident partner (Casier 2007: 82). When he became president, Putin granted a great deal of time to visiting Western European capitals highlighting the importance of economic relations with the EU. Putin's propensity for a more 'European' foreign policy was also explained by Moscow's attempt to counter US power and establish a multipolar world, where Russia was to be an equal partner to other super powers.

For its part, the EU continued to believe that the power of attraction of its values would generate successful economic transition and consolidate democracy in Russia. When, in 1999, nine European former communist countries met the Copenhagen criteria, thus becoming ready to start negotiations for EU accession, and

Putin's pro-European declarations seemed to be proof of the validity of this assumption (Light 2001: 21). The Common Strategy should have helped the EU and Russia to live 'in harmony together' while sharing the same common values. But its implementation had not even started in earnest when Brussels's cooperation with Moscow was again challenged.

In August 1999, Chechnya was transformed again into a bloody battlefield. It was motivated by Chechen rebel Shamyl Basayev's raids into Dagestan and bomb attacks on apartment blocks in different parts of Russia officially attributed to Chechen rebels but presented by, among others, journalist Anna Politkovskaya and exiled oligarch Boris Berezovsky as FSB-orchestrated terrorist acts for galvanising public support for a massive military action in Chechnya (Rosefielde and Hlouskova 2007: 218). Russia committed over 100,000 soldiers against a rebel force of a few thousand. Moreover, the Russian advance into Chechnya was heavily supported by the indiscriminate use of heavy artillery and air strikes. This tactic resulted in extensive civilian casualties that turned the issue into an international crisis, affecting Russia's relations with its Western partners (Haukkala 2010: 113).

The war reached its most severe phase in December 1999, when the Russian military delivered an ultimatum to the people of the Chechen capital — to leave the city or face annihilation. The siege of Groznyi coincided with a European Council meeting, as the EU was forced to do something. After long negotiations, the Council adopted the Declaration on Chechnya which condemned the intensive bombardments and outlined penalties and sanctions that might be applied to Russia, if it failed to change the conduct of the conflict (Forsberg 2005: 463).

In January 2000, the General Affairs Council decided to sanction Russia. The penalties — reduction of TACIS funding, and suspension of the signing of the Science and Technology Agreement — were rather modest and did not hurt Russia in any significant way. At first sight, this might seem surprising because in principle the EU had a vast array of measures at hand. In reality, the reason why the EU was not tough was largely because of the EU's own dependence on Russia: it could hardly afford to hit Russian exports as they consisted largely of oil, gas and other raw materials that the EU it-self needed. Moreover, by early 2000 rising oil prices on the world market ensured that Russia was no longer in need of short-term fi-nancial support from Western countries anymore (Haukkala 2010: 118).

Nevertheless, the Declaration on Chechnya and the sanctions were taken rather seriously in Moscow. The EU member states be-gan to hesitate and think that focusing too much and solely on the Chechen problem could risk politically alienating Moscow from the 'strategic partnership' with the EU. This thought, accompanied by an awareness of not being able to influence Russia's behaviour, gave rise to a more pragmatic interpretation of EU-Russian rela-tions (Haukkala 2010: 119). The member states became more reluc-tant to apply punitive measures against Russia and continued their bilateral dealings with Moscow, side-lining the Chechnya problem, while, at the EU level, European leaders still expressed disapproval of Russian actions.

In these conditions, it was not surprising that, at the EU sum-mit in Feira, in June 2000, the EU lifted sanctions it had adopted against Russia less than half a year ago. The decision was motivated by the EU's desire to create a good relationship with the new ad-ministration of president Putin. This justification was perplexing given that Putin had been *de facto* Russia's ruler since the launch of the second Chechen campaign (Forsberg 2005: 465).

Even though the sanctions were lifted, the European Council continued to call on Russia to avoid indiscriminate use of force, to cooperate with the OSCE, to ensure the delivery of humanitarian aid and to investigate human rights abuses. Thus, the EU aimed to maintain mutually beneficial cooperation with Russia while at the same time criticising it for violating 'common values' – a dual strat-egy that is designated in some of the academic literature as 'con-structive engagement'. The policy had to support the transfor-mation of Russia while preventing the self-imposed isolation of the country from the rest of Europe. Yet the result was not the expected one. The EU failed to win the kind of leverage over Russia that it was aiming at. Instead, the EU's post-sovereign agenda was dis-credited in the eyes of the Russians (Haukkala 2010: 124).

The EU's decision to lift the sanctions may have been motivated also by the pro-European declarations of Putin in the first few months of his presidency. Russia's reassertion of the importance of the relationship with the EU and its readiness for a strategic partnership with the Union, combined with Brussels' fear of alienating Moscow, increased by Russian elites and public support for the Chechen war, determined the EU to adopt the mentioned 'constructive engagement' strategy towards Russia. According to this strategy, the EU opted for close cooperation with Russia, despite the violations of 'common values', namely of human rights in Chechnya. This eventually caused substantial erosion of the value component in the post-sovereign logic of interaction in the EU-Russian relationship (Haukkala 2010: 129).

Even though the implementation of the PCA had witnessed serious problems (e.g. violation of human rights, lack of approximation of legislation and standards), the EU increased cooperation with Russia. At the EU-Russia summit in October 2000, Brussels launched the initiative of a Common European Economic Space (CEES) whose basic instruments were 'market opening', 'regulatory convergence' and 'trade facilitation'. The concept suited Putin's strategy to build a pragmatic mutually beneficial relationship with the EU and must be seen as the first instance of the new double strategy in action (Haukkala 2010: 130).

The attacks on 11 September 2001 transformed the context of the Chechen war. Moscow took advantage of this to legitimise its actions as part of the global war on terrorism. This Russian interpretation of the situation in Chechnya as an antiterrorist conflict rather than a separatist struggle was easily accepted by many EU member states (Forsberg 2005: 468). As a result, violation of human rights were holding increasingly less room on the agenda of EU-Russia summits after 11 September. EU leaders decided not to sacrifice political capital by raising the issue of Chechnya and human rights in order not to undermine the prospect of better relations with Russia (Forsberg 2005: 472), emphasising instead the importance of strategic partnership and energy dialogue. For the Kremlin, it was becoming easier to challenge international rules and reassert great-power status—especially now that growing revenues from the export of hydrocarbons offered the necessary prosperity and domestic stability.

2.1 The end of the 'Time of Troubles'

At the end of the 1990s, when Putin came to power, Russia was a weak country both internally and externally. Its economy was in free fall. Once feared, the Russian army was not able to win a conflict with a band of secessionists in Chechnya. The 1998 financial crisis resulted in the state's inability to pay public servants. Externally, Russia felt that it was not respected and its interests were ignored.

Against this background, the new president set his goal to re-create 'Great Russia' and make the country an important global actor. For this, however, Putin needed political and economic stability. And fortune smiled upon him: Putin's rise to power coincided with rising oil prices. In 1999, from a previous price of $10 per barrel, oil reached over $100 per barrel, quickly erasing the memory of catastrophic economic crisis in 1998. While oil exports brought the necessary money for enriching Russia and for paying foreign debts, natural gas and the monopoly on the pipelines that transport gas to the West transformed the country from an anaemic and almost broke state into a robust energy superpower (Goldman 2010: 136).

Economic growth was not pursued simply for its own sake but for the sake of enhancing political autonomy, and Russia's global position. Putin viewed the economic independence of Russia as a major prerequisite for a new role for the country on the world stage (Kanet 2007: 40). Therefore, for Moscow the payment of external debt was of paramount importance. It symbolised Russia's entry into the community of developed countries (Lo 2003: 55). With the economic recovery, Russia could claim again the status of a global superpower.

Regaining economic power and self-confidence, Moscow became more and more openly revisionist. The Kremlin decided that the price for European integration under Europe's conditions was too high. Russia felt that it had not been respected, that it had been exploited, ignored and victimised. Russia believed that laws are a mere expression of power and that, when the balance of power changes, laws should be changed unilaterally if needed to reflect it (Leonard and Popescu 2008: 20). Therefore, Moscow wanted to revise the international treaties signed during the Yeltsin period, because Russia was in a weaker position during the negotiations. It tried to revise commercial contracts with Western companies or military agreements such as, for example, the Treaty on Conventional Armed Forces in Europe. Russia claimed that it did nothing but correct a situation created by excessively generous concessions to Western interests granted by Yeltsin (Andréani 2008: 32).

The *smutnoe vremya* (Time of Troubles) — a paraphrase for the turbulent period of the early XVII century between the change of the Rurik and Romanovs dynasties, applied also to the chaos during Yeltsin's presidency — had ended. The enormous petrodollar revenues allowed Putin to stop internal reforms and to turn against the West after the US's invasion of Iraq. Putin restored order and solidified the state and cemented these successes, without real political and economic reforms. Now, the Kremlin felt that it did not need the West to achieve its objectives and could dictate the terms of cooperation.

Within this context, Russia felt insulted to be grouped together with Moldova, Morocco and other smaller states in the European Neighbourhood Policy (ENP), adopted in 2003. Instead of becoming part of the EU's neighbourhood, the Kremlin had insisted that its relations with the EU must be based on a separate basis of equal and mutually beneficial strategic partnership. The ENP aimed at creating, with the countries surrounding the EU, 'privileged relationships, building upon a mutual commitment to common values', mainly through bringing the partner states' legislation in line with the EU's *acquis communautaire*. Russia, however, saw the demand to coordinate its legislation with the principles of the *acquis communautaire* as interference in its internal affairs (Mankoff 2009: 159), to the extent that Moscow considered the EU was exporting its own values and rules not developed together with Russia. Moscow wanted an independent status in the international arena and, therefore, refused to be included in the ENP. The ENP only enhanced

Russia's determination to demand a more privileged status as a 'strategic partner' based on equality between both sides (Haukkala 2010: 134). The initiative of the Four Common Spaces at the St. Petersburg EU-Russia summit, in May 2003, was a response to Moscow's demands. Russia was given the option to 'choose not to participate' in the ENP. This concession, however, generated an important precedent: Even when cooperating with the EU within Europe one can 'choose to reject' political conditionality — a modification endangering the EU's external legitimacy (Malfliet and Partmentier 2010: 10).

The Four Common Spaces comprised the Common Economic Space covering not only economic issues, but also the environment, Common Space of Freedom, Security and Justice, Common Space of External Security including crisis management and non-proliferation, and Common Space of Research and Education including cultural aspects. They 'provided a framework for bringing Russia and the EU closer without the formalities of integration allowing Russia to maintain its position that it merited a special status on account of its size and importance' (Mankoff 2009: 160) and had to give a new impetus to EU-Russian relations. However, the negotiations for the road maps of the Four Common Spaces were not easy. They took two years and gave the EU many headaches.

The biggest problem concerned the very logic of the road maps. Russia wanted to treat the spaces separately, with individual action plans, so that the deals could be struck depending on the issue area in question — an approach which was unacceptable to the EU. Brussels accused Russia of a 'pick and choose' attitude of trying to comply with rules only in areas beneficial for itself while sidelining difficult issues and the EU's interests entirely (Haukkala 2010: 135). In the end, it was the EU that got its way and the four spaces remained a package deal. The road maps were adopted at the EU-Russia summit in Moscow, in May 2005.

In spite of the development of a formal institutional framework, generally, EU-Russian relations were not getting smoother. On the contrary, the EU's support for NATO intervention in Kosovo, in 1999, the serious violation of human rights during the Second Chechen war, the Yukos affair in 2003, and the strengthening

of authoritarianism in Russia, all increased the level of disagreement between the two partners. At the end of Putin's first term, it
was clear to the West that Russia would not become a democratic
country in the near future and that it could not be included in the
same group as Poland or even Ukraine (Trenin 2006: 91).

The EU's large 2004 enlargement further complicated the relationship with Russia. Officially, to be sure, Moscow's perception of
the process of expanding the European Union was positive—at
least, compared to the parallel NATO enlargement which was seen
as a US foreign policy instrument. The EU's eastern advance, however, increased the number of national interests and historical experiences within the European Union. Countries with no sympathy
for Russia became Union member states, bringing with them different issues of tension in the EU-Russian relationship. Even though
Poland's historic antipathy towards Russia or the status of ethnic
Russians in the Baltic states contributed to the cooling of relations
between the two partners, these facts, however, do not sustain the
Kremlin's interpretation that EU-Russian relations got worse only
after and because of the accession to the Union of Central and East
European 'russophobic' countries 'with an inferiority complex'. Rather, Brussels's criticism of Moscow had already grown in light of
the strengthening of authoritarianism in Russia before the EU's
2004 enlargement (Vahl 2007: 122).

Under President Putin, Russia abandoned the pretences of democratisation and re-established many of the institutional arrangements of traditional authoritarian political systems (Kanet 2009:
xvi). Under the pretext of restoring order, stabilising its economy
and re-establishing international grandeur, Putin strengthened central power, got rid of all those who repudiated his policies or were
concerned about the authoritarian state, reduced media freedom,
and manipulated the political system. With this approach, Putin received the support of a population afraid of crime, chaos and local
terrorism.

However, the 'colour revolutions' in the 'near abroad' threatened to jeopardise Putin's comfortable domestic situation. The
power of attraction of the democratic movements had the potential
to alienate the Russian population from its autocratic leadership.

Within this context, the Kremlin perceived the revolutions in Georgia, Ukraine and Kyrgyzstan, in 2003-2005, as a threat to the stability of the Russian Federation because of the possibility of diffusion. In the absence of any domestic justifications for the re-imposition of authoritarian political structures in Russia, the Kremlin focused on external threats (Kanet 2009: xvii). The West, in particular the United States, was presented as orchestrating the 'colour revolutions' in order to replace Moscow's influence in the former Soviet republics with Western domination. Moreover, the Ukrainian Orange Revolution was interpreted as a 'dress rehearsal for a regime change in Moscow' (Trenin 2011: 74). Consequently, Russia decided to take measures 'to protect' itself from 'external contamination'.

In May and July 2005 speeches, Vladislav Surkov, First Deputy Head of the Presidential Administration, introduced a new concept, which would come to define both Russian domestic and external policy (Umland 2016: 20). He stated that Russia's sovereignty was indirectly threatened by Western governments and NGOs, which use the language of human rights and democracy to undermine the stability of the Russian government and state, and that Russia must answer these criticisms and establish a political system protected from external pressures—a 'sovereign democracy' (Beachain 2010: 142). The concept was intended to protect the country from external pressure and ensure public support for the authoritarian system. In a short time, 'sovereign democracy' evolved into a new national ideology through which Russian domestic and foreign policy could be understood (Herd 2009: 3).

For the EU, one of the main aims of the relationship with Russia was the structural transformation of the country according to European norms, values, and models. The concept of 'sovereign democracy', however, implied that Russia's domestic policy concerned only Russia and that no external actor had any right to interfere. The concept espoused the intention of a democratic transition and ultimately the strengthening of democracy, with the crucial stipulation that this process should be based on Russia's own patterns. Russia alone would decide the 'democratic' rules it needs and would gradually implement structural reforms taking into account its historical and social features (Surkov 2006). Surkov suggested that 'sovereign democracy' reflected democracy in a sovereign state appealing to the 'dignity of the Russian people and Russian nation'. 'Sovereign democracy' is also an extension of patriotism, *derzhavnost'* (great power stateness), *sobornost'* (togetherness) and *pravoslavie* (orthodoxy), which reflect a long historical tradition of a centralised imperial state for whom it is more important to ensure order and stability than democracy (Herd 2009: 9). Looking through this prism, foreign actors are seen as trying to undermine Russia's territorial integrity and sovereignty for their own interests.

Another key element of the concept is that a state can obtain economic success and political stability without copying Western models. At the height of the oil and gas export-led economic boom, Russians started to view their country as more dynamic and economically successful than the EU. European norms and standards were seen as a source of dilution of Russia's sovereignty and incompatible with and even harmful to Russia's own economic trajectory (Haukkala 2010: 146). By conceptualising its economic success story as an ideological challenge to the West, Russia was deliberately reducing the common spaces and increasing the values gap with the EU. Thus, Russia's insistence on equality and respect for sovereignty led to a dilution of the principle of normative convergence envisaged int the Four Common Spaces, the consequent erosion of trust, and a downgrading the EU-Russian partnership to a limited cooperation (Baev 2008a: 294).

For Russia, it has since become imperative to 'keep and strengthen its sovereignty'. Moscow's new foreign policy started from the premise that a big country like Russia essentially does not have friends. Any other great power would not want a powerful Russia that could be a strong competitor. Instead, they would prefer a weak Russia that can be easily exploited and manipulated (Trenin 2006: 88). From Russia's point of view the EU's concerns with human rights and democratic values violations were perceived not as well-intended attempts to spread democratic norms, but as unacceptable interference in domestic affairs. Therefore, 'instead of adopting the norms and values promoted by the EU, Russia itself aspires to the role of a norm-maker' (Haukkala 2010: 103).

On several occasions Russia has questioned the legitimacy of European and international monitoring procedures and even embarked on a 'nationalisation of human rights'. A declaration, in this spirit, of the Chairman of Russia's Constitutional Court, Valery Zorkin, that Russia itself (and not the Strasbourg European Court on Human Rights) should resolve the problems with human rights of its citizens undermines European standards of human rights and the legitimacy of European institutions (Malfliet and Partmentier 2010: 16).

The EU's values were also questioned by the Russian Orthodox Church. During the World Council of the Russian People, in Moscow, in April 2006, then Metropolitan (and now Patriarch) Kirill read out his Declaration of Human Rights and Dignity. He condemned features of the Western lifestyle such as abortion, euthanasia and homosexuality, asserting that the Western concept of human rights was unsuitable for Russia. Instead, he emphasised faith, morality, sacred symbols and the concept of Motherland (*Mat' Rossia*) to fit the Russian national character (Baev 2008b: 39).

2.2   The economization of Russian foreign policy

To have political sovereignty, a state must have economic independence and military security. Russia's need to be economically powerful and independent generated a strategy of limiting foreign investment in basic economic sectors such as energy, pipelines, telecommunications, road and rail infrastructure, military industry and finance, and an economisation of its foreign policy. This means 'the use of energy independence and economic stimulus and sanctions to assert Russia's economic and foreign policy goals' (Meister 2010: 2).

For Moscow, the revenues from the oil and gas industry ensured the stability of the political regime and represented the main instrument of its geopolitical influence. A specialist in natural resources, with a scholarly dissertation defended at the St Petersburg Mining Institute entitled 'Strategic planning of the production of mineral-natural bases in the region under the development of market economy conditions', Putin's philosophy is that energy policy and energy security are essential to Russia's security policy. The soaring prices of gas and oil made energy-rich Russia more powerful, less cooperative and more intransigent. Moscow was trying to take advantage of the growing European demand for gas and establish a relationship of asymmetric interdependence with the EU, a situation where the EU needs Russia more than Russia needs the EU (Leonard and Popescu 2007). However, the more gas the EU bought from Russia, the more Russia became dependent on the EU market. This generated a paradox: The closer Russia and the EU came territorially or economically, the more problematic their relationship became. Interdependence and proximity developed into a constant source of frustration (Medvedev 2008: 217).

The economisation of foreign policy strengthened Russia but also affected relations with its neighbours. In the absence of any ideology or common *acquis*, the CIS countries kept close relations with Russia due to their economic benefits. The decision to raise prices on the energy exported to the former Soviet republics close to the levels of current deals with EU member states reduced Russia's allure, and made closer relationships with the West increasingly attractive for Russian neighbours. However, dominated by a realist perception of international relations, Moscow could not accept the loss of its 'spheres of interests'. As a result, the relations with common neighbours became the prime area of EU-Russian tensions (Debardeleben 2009: 98).

2006 was a year of trade wars in Russia's relations with the EU and the 'near abroad'. At the beginning of January, the 'gas war' between Russia and Ukraine reduced gas supplies to EU members. Later the relationship with the EU was complicated by Russia's refusal to ratify the European Energy Charter and its ban on wine imports from Moldova and Georgia. In November, during the EU-Russia summit, the negotiations for a new PCA could not be started because of Poland's veto, which protested against a Russian ban on Polish meat imports. It all culminated on 1 January 2007, when Russia threatened to suspend food imports from the EU, under the pretext that two new member states, Romania and Bulgaria, did not comply with some phytosanitary requirements. All these frictions showed that EU-Russian relations were dominated by distrust, mutual frustration and a general institutional stalemate, which produced continuous disputes (Medvedev 2008: 216).

Russia's growingly aggressive stance towards the EU became obvious at the Munich Conference on Security Policy, in February 2007, when the Russian president openly expressed dissatisfaction with what he considered double standards and differential treatment. Putin highlighted Russia's greatness, its history 'that spans more than a thousand years' and therefore its 'privilege to carry out an independent foreign policy' (Putin 2007b). Russia had regained its confidence and pride in its Tsarist and Soviet past. In another famous speech in 2005, in the State Duma, Putin had declared that the collapse of the Soviet Union was 'the biggest geopolitical catastrophe' of the 20th century. Russia had no longer to prove that it was a great power — it *was* a great power and this meant that it had the right to follow its own interests without taking into account others' opinions.

With the worsening of the relationship with Brussels, Moscow's scepticism towards the EU as an organisation increased. Accordingly, Russia preferred legally binding comprehensive bilateral relations with the Union's member states rather than with the EU as a whole (Yurgens 2010: 21). This tactic had and has several advantages, from a Russian viewpoint. It fits Moscow's belief in the supremacy of the state and distrust of law and international organisations. States can at least be expected to act in their national interest and to be less moralistic about democracy, human rights, and so on than the EU as a whole (Mankoff 2009: 14).

As Moscow seeks to portray itself as one of the Great Powers in Europe, it prefers to conduct its business with its equals — mainly Britain, France and Germany — while side-lining the EU institutions and smaller member states in the process, if it can (Haukkala 2010: 108). A preference for such bilateralism is clearly stated in the Foreign Policy Concept of the Russian Federation:

> 'The development of mutually advantageous bilateral relationships with Germany, France, Italy, Spain, Finland, Greece, the Netherlands, Norway and some other West-European

States is an important resource for promoting Russia's national interests in European and world affairs' (*Kontseptsiya vneshney politiki Rossisyskoy Federatsyi* 1999) and is part of traditional international relations based on material interests and bargaining.

The preference for bilateral relations and the lack of trust in institutions often give the impression that Russia plays EU member states off against one another. 'But Russia can hardly be blamed for such behaviour when some in Europe appear to invite it and fail to deliver a unified message' (Mandelson 2007). Leonard and Popescu (2007: 2) have identified five distinct policy approaches to Russia, within the EU member states:

- 'Trojan Horses' (Cyprus and Greece) which are defenders of Russian interests in the EU,
- 'Strategic Partners' (France, Germany, Italy and Spain) that have a 'special relationship' with Russia,
- 'Friendly Pragmatists' (Austria, Belgium, Bulgaria, Finland, Hungary, Luxembourg, Malta, Portugal, Slovakia and Slovenia) with close relationships with Russia and a tendency to put business interests above political values,
- 'Frosty Pragmatists' (Czech Republic, Denmark, Estonia, Ireland, Latvia, Netherlands, Romania, Sweden, United Kingdom) guided by business interests, but less afraid than others to speak out against Russian behaviour on human rights or other issues concerning the rule of law, and
- 'New Cold Warriors' (Lithuania and Poland) with an overtly hostile approach towards Moscow.

Disunity among Union members makes EU-Russian negotiations slow and complicated further encouraging Moscow's bilateralism.

The growth of bilateral arrangements has, on the whole, increased Russian bargaining leverage, allowing the Kremlin to play different European states off against each other and limiting the range of issues where Russia finds itself confronting a solid European bloc (Mankoff 2009: 151). The bilateralist temptation discourages Russia from adopting common values as well as from continuing the democratisation process of the country; it makes cooperation with the EU more difficult. For Putin, national interest is more important than compliance with European principles, rules and values assumed voluntarily. Thus, during his first two presidential terms, Russia became more assertive in pursuing its foreign and security policy objectives and showed that it no longer needed even to pretend to accept the normative policy prescriptions of its Western neighbours as a precondition for normalising its relationship with them (Kanet 2009: 239).

Russia's authoritarian drift, tensions over the expansion of NATO, Moscow's interference in the affairs of its neighbours, and disputes over Russian energy supplies to Europe led to a significant deterioration of EU-Russia relations during the latter years of Putin's second presidential mandate (Mankoff 2009: 145). This worsening trend reached its peak in August 2008 when, for the first time since the fall of the USSR, Russia invaded another state. And for the first time in history two members of the Council of Europe fought against each other in a war.

Conclusions

In contrast to widespread assumption that EU-Russia relations worsened only with Putin's presidency, the present chapter demonstrates that cooperation between Moscow and Brussels has never been very smooth. The apparent propensity to democratization and shared European values at the beginning of '90s was merely a result of confusion and anxiety of the former communist political elite. In the absence of a new ideology and an external enemy as well as facing a serious economic crisis and rampant criminality, Russia saw the rapprochement with the West as a solution for its problems. However, the EU-Russia 'honeymoon' did not last long. The 1993 political crisis and the first Chechen War showed Europe that Russia was not going to follow the same path as the East-Central European countries did.

Russia's 'weakness power' made the EU turn a blind eye to her deviations from the democratic principles, in order to 'lock the country into an institutional arrangement' and to prevent 'the roll-back of Russian democracy and economic reforms' (Haukkala

2010). This strategy, however, was undermining the EU's normative power. It encouraged Russia to challenge European values, a trend that became more pronounced with Putin's coming to power.

As a result of the increasing oil price and rising state revenues, Russia was able to pay back foreign debt, and to strengthen the central power of the state. Externally, the Kremlin's claim of 'great powerness' (*velikoderzhavnost'*) became more persistent. Compliance with European norms and values was seen as a dilution of sovereignty. Democratic reforms were associated with the chaos of Yeltsin's period. It became a matter of pride that Russia would no longer accept 'instructions' from Washington or Brussels. Moreover, the EU's increasing gas demand allowed Moscow to use hydrocarbons for leverage against European countries. If we add to these aspects Russia's growing interests for the former Soviet republics and her approach to them in terms of zero-sum games, we have a complete picture of EU-Russia relations on the eve of Georgian War.

Yet, the negative evolution of EU-Russia relations should not be attributed only to the Kremlin's decisions and measures taken during Yeltsin's and Putin's presidencies. The EU's ignorance or lack of firmness vis-à-vis Russia's avoidance to comply with voluntary assumed European rules and values encouraged both presidents who led Russia from the Cold War to the Georgian War to depart from democratic reforms and common values whenever they considered state interests, the pride of Great Russia or the strength of central power as being endangered. Indeed, it became harder to sanction Russia when the country recovered from economic disaster and became aware of its importance as gas supplier.

Chapter 3
Crossing the Red Line: The EU and Russia within the Contexts of the Georgian War and Ukraine Crisis

Introduction

Since the collapse of the Soviet Union, Russian foreign policy has been informed by the debate of two fundamentally opposed directions: whether the national interests are better served by rapprochement with, and ultimate integration into, the Euro-Atlantic community, or whether Russia should seek to follow its own way (i.e. reintegration of the northern Eurasian space) and to constrain the exercise of US power around the globe (Gvosdev and Marsh 2014: 54). Oscillation between these two approaches can be observed in Russian foreign policy after 2009 as well.

Moscow is still afraid of remaining isolated in the international arena, of not being a voice heard in global affairs (see Chapter 1) and therefore, seeks good relations with other international actors, in particular with the EU, for its economic development, the credibility of its foreign policy, and the security of the region. In the logic of balance of power, the EU is seen as a 'useful' counterbalance to the hegemonic US, that 'has overstepped its national borders in every way [imposing its] economic, political, cultural and educational policies [...] on other nations (Purin 2007). This explains why, during the Georgian War, Russia was more open for mediation by the EU than any other international actor, in particular NATO and the US. Moscow reacted positively to a peace proposal of French President Nicolas Sarkozy, and ultimately agreed to a solution that ended the August 2008 war (Kobrinskaya 2009: 21). The decision to accept Paris as an interlocutor was not at random. In August 2008 France was presiding the Council of the European Union and Moscow's rapprochement with Paris was conformed with Russia's overall approach toward the EU as a counterweight to the USA.

1.   Rebuilding international credibility

Promoter of collective security, interdependence and cooperation between states on the basis of commonly accepted norms and rules, the August 2008 war in Georgia came as a shock for the West. The events in the Caucasus questioned not only the reliability of the Kremlin as a partner on the international arena, but also the West's policies of integrating Russia in the European community of values. Neither for Moscow the new context was comfortable. Risking international isolation and dependent on the European market, the Kremlin needed to clean up its image abroad and reassure the EU member states of its good intentions. As such, in the immediate aftermath of the Georgian war, Moscow shaped its foreign policy efforts towards 'placating' first of all the EU. Russia started deliberately with the East-Central European EU members, due to the fact that, in 2008, there were Poland and Lithuania that blocked negotiations for a new EU-Russia Partnership and Cooperation Agreement.

Vladimir Putin seems to have realised that without normal Polish-Russian relations there can be no normal relations with the EU as a whole (Trenin 2010a). Therefore, the Russian Prime Minister came to Poland in 2009 to attend the solemn ceremony commemorating the 70th anniversary of the start of World War II. After that, Putin invited Polish Prime Minister Donald Tusk to come to Katyn in April 2010 for a joint ceremony to honour the death of Polish officers 70 years earlier. Putin even kneeled, briefly, while laying a wreath to the memorial—a gesture that was much appreciated (Trenin 2010b).

Polish-Russian relations were put to the severest test three days later, when the Polish presidential plane crashed at Smolensk. For the first time in living memory, Russia declared a national day of mourning to honour the foreign dead (Trenin 2010b). President Medvedev went to the funeral and clearly named Stalin as responsible for the murders at Katyn. Moscow did not react to the accusations made by some Poles that it might have been involved in the Smolensk air crash. Eventually, Russia was pleased with the following Polish elections results.

Besides the 'image exercise' in Poland, Russia signed with France a contract of acquisition of two Mistral warships worth 1,2 billion euros. The deal, concluded shortly after the war in Georgia with the country that negotiated the peace proposal, demonstrated that Russia had opened a new phase in relations with Western Europe. The cost of the Mistral ships seemed to be a low price that Russia was willing to pay for a considerable political success, in the context of the atmosphere of mistrust in its relations with the West (Zochowski 2010: 4).

Moscow made important moves in other domains too. Considering that the most important issue of disagreement between Russia and the EU and an essential element of the PCA agreement (Haukkala 2010: 84) represented respect for human rights, in February 2010, Russia ratified Protocol 14 of the European Convention of Human Rights. Of the 47 member states of the Council of Europe, Russia had been the last to ratify the protocol, after four years of hesitation. The delay was widely interpreted as a blocking tactic, undermining the Court from functioning effectively and thus the cause of human rights in Europe (Emerson 2010).

This and similar gestures have not led to major changes for Russian citizens though. As, among others, the 2011 parliamentary elections and Putin's third presidential term would show, the Kremlin remained unwilling to resume democratization of the country. Instead, Russia usually makes some concessions for pleasing Western partners. However, when criticized for a lack of democracy, the Kremlin keeps underlining that Russia builds on its own traditions and will develop them in its own ways and at its own pace (Kanet 2007: 15–16). Furthermore, Moscow accuses the EU of attempting to meddle in its domestic affairs, by trying to enforce its own legislation as a condition for cooperation (Kulhanek 2010: 56) - in contradiction with Russia's notions of independence and great power status.

To be sure, the EU-Russia relationship may still be built on the assumption of the existence of similar values and goals between the parties (Haukkala 2010: 2). However, Russia is insisting on its sovereign right to pick and choose the right combination of reforms as well as to decide on how best to implement the reforms to suit its own needs. The Foreign Policy Concept is full of references to the importance of preserving, enhancing and buttressing Russian sovereignty (Haukkala 2010: 105). With a formally democratic constitution, yet rather peculiar interpretation of the rule of law, it is little wonder that, in *The Economist's* Democracy Index, Russia's political system was, in 2010, downgraded from its previous status as a 'hybrid regime' (Economist Intelligent Unit 2010). As a now 'authoritarian state', it assumed the world's 107th place in the Democracy Index. If fell further to the 117th place in 2011 and 134th place in 2016.

Apart from the issue of human rights and the rule of law, energy relations with Russia give EU's leaders their biggest headaches. This state of affairs is rooted in the importance of the energy sector for Russian internal and external policy. For Moscow, the revenues from the oil and gas industries ensure the stability of the political regime and represent the main instruments of its geopolitical influence. The immense reserves of hydrocarbons are not seen by Moscow through the lenses of liberal win-win principle but as an instrument that confers Russia a great leverage in the game of balance of power. Within this context, the 'energodiplomacy' that emerged in Putin's first presidential term has since dominated EU-Russia relations.

Despite Russia's political narrative implying a dominant position, as a basic feature, EU-Russian energy relations are characterised by strong mutual dependence. Russia is the EU's biggest energy supplier and the EU is Russia's biggest trading partner. Moreover, even though the Kremlin has been trying to increase Europe's dependence on its energy, Russia may actually need the EU more than Brussels needs Moscow. While some member states are unduly dependent on Russian energy and a few alarmingly so (e.g. Finland, the Baltic states, Bulgaria), the EU as a whole does not suffer from excessive dependency upon Russia. Russian fuel exported to the EU represent over three quarters of all its exports. For the EU, however, these constitute less than one third of its total energy import needs (Polish-Russian Group on Difficult Matters 2011).

Under these conditions, the EU would be able to withstand an interruption in imports of crude oil or natural gas from Russia because the EU's energy consumption could be replaced by other energy sources (nuclear, renewable, liquefied gas) and suppliers, i.e. via increased imports of Norwegian, Middle Eastern and Nigerian gas or increased imports of Saudi oil. Russia's position would thus be vulnerable if the EU decided to reduce its purchases of Russian oil and gas. In this scenario, Russia would be threatened with financial collapse due to its inability to replace lost revenue (Tichy 2010: 6). This mutual dependence between Russia and Europe has meant that Russia's energy weapon has, in fact, turned out to be less potent that some in the Kremlin may have hoped for, and that many Europeans have been fearing (Mankoff 2009: 178).

The January 2009 Ukrainian gas crisis, Russia's withdrawal from the Energy Treaty, the Arab revolts in North Africa, and the Japanese earthquake, tsunami and nuclear accident, which called into question the reliability of nuclear energy, have put in question the security of European energy supplies. However, the EU has since been trying to overcome these challenges. Thus, in order to reduce its import vulnerability, in November 2010, the European Commission adopted a ten-year Energy plan titled *Energy 2020: A Strategy for Competitive, Sustainable and Secure Energy.*

The Commission's objectives for 2020 are to increase the share of renewable energy to 20% and to make a 20% improvement in energy efficiency. The large EU members of Western Europe are less dependent on Russian imports, while the countries of East-Central Europe have fewer alternatives and are from 70% to 99% dependent on gas and oil imports from Russia. The strategy thus involves an obligation of solidarity among member states, internal infrastructure development and creating interconnections across external borders and maritime areas. This way, gas could circulate in case of a crisis and transferred from one country to another.

The EU also puts an important accent on modernisation of the existing infrastructure, with specific emphasis on the Southern Corridor. Europe has also found different sources of energy in Qatar and even in the USA, i.e. countries now exporting liquefied gas. In January 2011, the EU and Azerbaijan signed an agreement on natural gas supplies, which commits Azerbaijan to selling 'substantial volumes of gas over the long term' to the EU (Pannier 2011). The agreement represents a first firm commitment from a Caspian Basin country to providing gas for the EU's Southern Corridor. It showed concrete results already at the end of June 2013, when the consortium managing the offshore Shah Deniz gas field in Azerbaijan announced its selection of the Trans-Adriatic Pipeline (TAP) for the delivery of Caspian gas to the EU.

Moscow perceives this EU policy as a threat to its foreign energy policies (Tichy 2010: 21) and has reacted defensively. A week after the signing of the EU-Azerbaijan agreement on the Southern Corridor, Gazprom announced that it would increase the amount of gas it purchases from Azerbaijan, in order to make the European project nonviable because of a lack of sufficient hydrocarbon reserves. Russia has been also trying to diversify its energy exports and reduce its dependence on the EU market by opening an Asian route to Chinese, Korean and Japanese markets. In 2014, Moscow signed two gas deals with Beijing seemingly suggesting a switch of its major gas export direction from Europe to Asia.

However, even though these agreements theoretically offer Russia a stronger bargaining power in its energy relations with the EU, the size and significance of the Russian gas deliveries to China are distant and uncertain. The flow of Russian gas to China will not commence until 2018 and could reach an amount of 38 billion cubic meters annually only after 30 years (Rotaru 2016: 38). Thus, Russia remains dependent on the EU as its most lucrative market for Russia. Gazprom makes nearly 70% of its profits from sales to the EU (Talus 2010: 33).

In addition, Russia faces further challenges with regard to its Chinese neighbourhood, such as the demographic discrepancies between underpopulated Siberia and overpopulated China. According to some experts, 'Vladivostok is already a Chinese city, both economically and culturally and the Chinese make up more than half the population of Khabarovsk' (Barysch 2011: 25). As such, Russia is more and more concerned about the exposure of its thinly populated Far East to the rising power of China.

Beijing's growing involvement in Central Asia including the launch of a gas pipeline from Turkmenistan to China via Uzbeki-

stan and Kazakhstan, as well as Turkmenistan's thriving cooperation with Iran have seriously limited Gazprom's ability to have
Central Asian gas at its disposal (Paszyc 2010). Furthermore, Moscow fears being marginalised in a world where power and wealth
oscillate between Asia and the Pacific. It will be needing allies to
counter-balance growing Chinese power along its Asian border.
Thus, at least in the medium term, Russia is 'condemned' to have
the EU as its main partner in the energy field.

The asymmetric interdependency between Russia and the EU
is obvious in trade in general. The EU is the most important Russian
commercial partner, while Russia is ranked third among the EU's
trading partners, after the US and China. More than half of Russia's
trade is conducted with EU states, and 75% of foreign direct investment in Russia comes from the EU (Cwiek-Kaprovicz 2010). On the
other side, the EU's exports to Russia represent up to 6% of the total
value of its exports. Russia accounts for around 10% of the EU's imports (Polish-Russian Group of Difficult Matters 2011: 5). Thus,
Russia is more dependent on the EU than vice versa (Barysch 2011:
30).

Russia's dependency on trade with, especially energy exports
to, the EU could further increase given such new and future projects
as Nord Stream I and II via the Baltic Sea to Germany and Turk
Stream via Turkey to the Balkans. Russia has sought to enhance its
leverage over Europe through construction of new pipelines and to
change the asymmetric interdependence to its advantage, that is to
make Europe more dependent on Russia than Russia is on the EU.
However, these pipelines not only increase the sheer quantity of oil
and gas Russia can export to Europe, but also increase Russia's dependency on the European market.

2.   In search of modernisation without democratisation

Soaring oil and gas prices have provided more state income for
strengthening governmental institutions and ensuring a degree of
prosperity for Russian citizens. However, the energy resources
have proved to be both a blessing and a curse for the country. Be-
witched by huge revenues from the sale of hydrocarbons, Russian

authorities have been refusing to address the real needs of the country.

The aftermath of the Georgian War and even more so of the Ukraine Crisis proved how fragile Russian prosperity is. The stock market lost close to half its total value in barely a month, and trading had to be halted repeatedly in the autumn of 2008 to avoid greater damage. With the beginning of the global recession, oil prices dropped from over $140 a barrel to below $50 (Mankoff 2009: 304). Russia realised that its economy based on the export of raw materials (oil, gas, steel) is sustainable. The Soviet Union collapsed as a result of, among other factors, of the fall of the oil price on world markets, in the mid-1980s. Post-Soviet Russia was on the verge of collapse at the beginning of the 1990s when the oil price fell to $10 per barrel (Stürmer 2011: 72). These Russian experiences had demonstrated that an economy based on the export of hydrocarbons cannot guarantee the security of the country. Modernisation, so it seemed, was required. Putin had already acknowledged this when, in 2006, he told the Security Council that 'the level of military security depends directly on the pace of economic growth and technological development' (Mankoff 2009: 33).

Within tis context, there is no wonder that the need for economic modernisation became one of the top priorities of President Medvedev's policies:

'Creating favourable external conditions for the modernisation of Russia, transformation of its economy through innovation, enhancement of living standards, consolidation of society, strengthening of the foundations of the constitutional system, rule of law and democratic institutions, realisation of human rights and freedoms and, as a consequence, ensuring national competitiveness in a globalising world' (as quoted in Mankoff 2009: 13).

However, to develop its economy, Russia needed advanced machinery and technology even for the extraction of raw materials. Such machinery can be found in the West and predominantly in Europe. As such, the importance of Russia's relationship with the EU grew.

The other side, the EU was aware that it needed Russia to be prosperous, stable and at peace with itself and its neighbours, a chaotic, angry and unstable Russia being a risk to EU security and prosperity (Polish-Russian Group of Difficult Matters 2011: 5). Embedded in liberal institutionalist thinking that support the idea that the economic interdependence of international actors pushes them not only towards cooperation in economic area but approaches them also to normative principles of peace, freedom and democracy; the EU was willing to improve the economic relationship with Russia. Thus, during the EU-Russia summit at Rostov-on-Don (31 May–1 June 1 2010), as a response to Moscow's needs, the EU launched the Partnership for Modernisation. The agreement promoted a sustainable low-carbon economy and energy efficiency, and cooperation in innovation, research and development. The EU hoped that the Partnership would lead to political liberalisation in Russia in addition to economic growth. As Katinka Barysh put it,

'indirectly a modernisation partnership could contribute to the EU's ultimate aim: to make Russia more democratic, accountable and open. In the medium term, successful modernisation could help to transform an apathetic Russian middle class into an entrepreneurial class that demands property rights and civil liberties' (Barysch 2010: 28).

For the EU only a democratic Russia, which conforms to the rule of law, can be a reliable partner. That is why the EU's interests towards Russia lie in the spheres of transformation, Westernisation and cooperation (Romaniuk 2009: 71).

However, Moscow has been more interested in a narrower modernisation plan, focused mainly on technology transfer, support for innovative industries and other state-led interventions without social, political, and economic reforms. Moscow has insisted that primarily economic purposes should be incorporated into the EU-Russia modernisation partnership. Russian officials made clear that the Partnership for Modernisation 'should direct attention to practical questions rather than to benefits of European values' as declared by Vladimir Chizov, Russia's EU representative, supported by Sergei Lavrov, the Russian foreign minister: 'We intend to give precedence to the most concrete and significant questions, including the economy, social problems, education, science, technology, innovation' (as quoted in Adomeit 2011: 41).

Yet can modernisation take place without democratisation? Can one have business development without a proper and stable legal framework? Contrary the rhetoric during Putin's and Medvedev's tenures of office, the problem of corruption has significantly increased rather than lessened. This has been a barrier to modernisation as corruption is anathema to fair competition and it removes potential funds of investment from the economy (Adomeit 2011: 41). Thus, according to Transparency International, Russia was in 2010 in 154th place, out of a total of 178, on the organisation's corruption index (Transparency International 2010).

The lack of democratic reforms, disrespect for human rights and rule of law created another important obstacle to modernisation of the country: human capital flight. About a million and a half Russians are estimated to have emigrated in just three years. Research and development efforts suffer from significant 'brain drain'. Russian talent prefers to go abroad rather than stay at home not primarily because of financial reasons, but because of the freedom, opportunities and better lifestyle they are able to enjoy in Europe and the US (Adomeit 2011: 49)·

The Kremlin's obstinacy in not complying with democratic principles has impeded not only the Partnership for Modernisation but runs also contrary to the mentioned four 'Common Spaces' agreed upon at the EU-Russian St. Petersburg Summit in May 2003. Brussels and Moscow had agreed to reinforce their cooperation by creating four long term 'common spaces' in the framework of the Partnership and Cooperation Agreement and on the basis of common values and shared interests, the common economic space covering economic issues and the environment, common space of freedom, security and justice, common space of external security that includes crisis management and non-proliferation, and common space of research and education which includes cultural aspects.

Against the background of their difficult implementation, there is little wonder why the negotiations for the new PCA between the EU and Russia were difficult. Russia increasingly

avoided entering into firm legal relations with the EU, instead preferring a wide open legal frame generating loose obligations (Yurgens 2010: 21). President Medvedev argued for replacing the old
PCA, which expired in 2007, with an essentially technical agreement focusing primarily on economic cooperation, while the EU favours more detailed arrangements with special emphasis on energy
and security issues. Many East Europeans also would like the
agreement to be focused on human rights and Russia's relations
with neighbouring (non-EU) states such as Georgia, Ukraine or the
Republic of Moldova. They inserted a clause into the EU negotia-
tors' instructions that resolving the 'frozen conflicts' around Russia's borders should be a priority in EU-Russian relations (Mankoff
2009: 160).

As Brussels could not put more pressure on Moscow to respect
democratic values and could not make domestic changes hapen in
Russia, she also cannot become part of the community of European
values. Her participation in the European integration process
would have been only be superficial. Thus, while Russia induced
the idea that Brussels was delaying the signing of a new Partnership
Cooperation Agreement or PCA 2, the key was always in Moscow's
hands. The EU could not go ahead with a PCA 2 against the background that the four common spaces were not being taken seriously
by Russia.

3.   Contesting the EU

Putin's return to the Kremlin for the third presidential term in 2012
brought important changes in Russia's relations with the EU. In October 2011, less than a week after the second Eastern Partnership
Summit, Vladimir Putin had announced his plans for the former
Soviet space — which would later be labelled the Eurasian Economic
Union (EEU). His vision implied more than a regional economic integration project, seeking rather to divide the continent in two
spaces where the Russia-led EEU would be a co-equal of the EU and
where both unions could create then a joint European economic
space from Lisbon to Vladivostok. This way Russia would

strengthen its international position and would place its interpretation of norms and values on the same foot as the EU's *acquis communautaire* (Lo 2015: 181).

Equal footing in relations to the West in the area of values was asserted by Putin in particular during the 2011–2012 Russian domestic protests and later during the Ukraine crisis starting in late 2013. Besides accusing Western countries of organizing 'colour revolutions', Putin's discourse suggested that both the EU and the US are trying to impose alien values on the former Soviet space. He was emphasizing that, in fact, the basis of the European civilization should not come from the EU's normative monopoly and the *acquis communautaire*, but from where you feel to be European (Lo 2015: 181).

The Kremlin's rhetoric became more radical towards the EU's norms and values in the second part of 2013. Vladimir Putin accused Western Europe of decadence and of being in a deep moral crisis, depicting, on the other side, Russia as the last defender of conservative Christian values. This stance towards the EU contributed to disillusionment and mutual distrust between the two parts. As Liliya Shevtsova commented at the time, relations between Russia and the EU were dominated, already by the end of 2013, by 'mutual frustration, disappointment and even disgust regarding each other' (House of Lords 2014).

Russia was perceiving the EU more and more as an adversarial competitor in their common neighbourhood and was trying to divert the former Soviet republics from progressing within the framework of the EaP. Within this context, Armenia's sudden decision, in September 2013, to join the EEU instead of initialling the Association Agreement (AA) with the EU was seen by Russia as a clear geopolitical victory. Moscow showed Brussels how easily it can 'convince' the former soviet republics to reconsider their rapprochement with the EU and how strong its leverage towards the former Soviet republics was.

In the light of its zero-sum perception of competition with the West in Russia's 'near abroad', the Kremlin tried to make other neighbours change their mind about initialling or signing association agreements with the EU as well. Above all, Moscow put economic pressure on both Moldova and Ukraine. The Russian president accused the EU of blackmailing Kyiv to sign the AA, threatening it with mass protests (BBC 2013). Eventually Moscow succeeded in convincing Ukrainian President Yanukovych with promises of subsidies and loans not to sign the agreement with the EU. However, what Moscow had not anticipated was the reaction of the Ukrainian society.

The Euromaidan protests were interpreted by Russia as a Western orchestrated *coup d'etat*. As a reaction, Moscow intensified criticism on the EU. After the EU's foreign policy chief Catherine Ashton and the German foreign minister visited the protestors on the Independence Square in Kyiv at the beginning of December 2013, Russian foreign minister Lavrov called these visits 'indecent' and assessed the situation in Ukraine as 'getting out of control' (BBC 2014).

Eventually, EU-Russia relations reached the lowest level after Russia's subsequent intervention in, and then annexation of, Crimea. On 6 March 2014, the EU heads of state and government announced the suspension of the negotiations on the new EU-Russia PCA and of the meetings at the highest political level (the last EU-Russia summit had taken place on 28 January 2014 in Brussels). The EU also joined the US in imposing travel bans on individuals and officials responsible with the annexation of Crimea and economic sanctions on Russian and Crimean entities and individuals.

The annexation of Crimea by the Russian Federation precipitated the signing of the Association Agreements of Ukraine, Moldova and Georgia with the EU. Symbolically, on 21 March 2014, the very day Vladimir Putin signed the Crimea annexation law, the EU signed the political part of the Association Agreement with Ukraine. Despite Russian economic pressure on the eastern partners, on 27 June 2014, Brussels signed the DCFTA with Ukraine and the AA with Moldova and Georgia.

Russia's instigation of, and later open intervention in, the war in Eastern Ukraine and the shooting down, on 17th July 2014, by a Russian missile, of Malaysia Airline flight MH17 with 298 dead people, the great majority of whom were EU citizens, among them 193 Dutch, determined EU leaders to develop a more robust stance towards Moscow. In July-September 2014, the EU and the US imposed a new package of economic sanctions on Russia. In response, on 6 August 2014, Moscow imposed an import embargo on numerous agricultural products from the EU. This strongly affected European food and drinks exports, Russia being Europe's second largest consumer market for these products.

The 13 November 2015 Paris terrorist attacks provided Russia with an opportunity to reset its relations with the EU. Moscow pointed out its indispensability in the fight against the terrorism and its important role in ensuring EU's security. Brussels has answered according Russia's expectations. On 18 November 2015, the president of EU Commission, Jean-Claude Junker, declared that 'there is no security architecture in Europe without an enhanced participation of Russia' and that 'USA, Russia and Europe, should work together when it comes to fight the scourge of Islamic State' (Euractiv 2015). Yet, the mutual sanctions are still in place.

Conclusions

After a quarter of century since the collapse of the Soviet Union, the Kremlin still perceives foreign policy to a significant degree as a zero-sum power game, where the West tries to expand its spheres of influence into the Russian area of 'privileged interest'. Yet, the EU still expects that Russia's traditional worldview will change sooner or later, convinced that zero sum-games are too expensive in the present international order, and that the concept of sovereign democracy runs against the very logic of globalisation and cannot be sustained. The conviction in Brussels is that Russia has no other option but to 'adapt' to the new international order, where stability and prosperity are better guaranteed through sharing the same universal values: rule of law, human rights, and democratic liberties. As Keukeleire and MacNaughtan (2008: 8) argue, if the world is different, foreign policy can no longer be based on the conventional state and (military) power-centered concepts of foreign policy from the previous era. Moscow's obsession with security, independence and national interest only demonstrate that, although Russia may be a great power it is not an 'up-dated' one open to international integration but a power that sees the world through traditional lenses of 19th and 20th century realism.

The National Security Strategy (NSS) of the Russian Federation until 2020, ratified by Dmitri Medvedev in May 2009, clearly specifies that Russia aims to play an important role in the world together with the US, China and other great powers and to act as a hegemon in the post-Soviet space. However, Russia still needs the EU in several ways. To be fully acknowledged as an important power by the international community, the Kremlin longs for full recognition by the West (Casier 2011:543). As Russia's relations with the USA are often strained, the EU represents, in some ways, a guarantor of Russia's status, in the international arena.

Moscow and Brussels need each other both in terms of security and economically, the sanctions imposed after the annexation of Crimea affecting both parts. Yet Russia's energy policy, authoritarianism, and the violation of the sovereignty and territorial integrity of its neighbours have all limited its ability to seek fuller integration with the evolving institutional web of Europe (Mankoff 2009: 182). The EU-Russian partnership holds a lot of potential for a win-win situation. Both continue to need each other: Russia to avoid isolation and export its goods, the EU to secure its energy supplies and stability on its Eastern borders (Casier 2011: 86). However, Russia should stop perceiving EU policies through zero-sum lenses. As both Brussels and Moscow seek a stable neighbourhood, European initiatives should not be perceived as challenges, but as opportunities for further cooperation. The European Union is strongly interested in deepening and widening cooperation with Russia. However, the international agreements, the rule of law and democratic rights cannot be set-aside during dialogue with Moscow.

Part II
A Partnership for a Common Neighbourhood

Chapter 4
From the 'New Neighbourhood Initiative' to the Eastern Partnership

Introduction

On 7 May 2009, EU leaders and the representatives of six former Soviet republics, Armenia, Azerbaijan, Belarus, Georgia, Moldova and Ukraine, met in Prague to sign a cooperation agreement labelled as the Eastern Partnership (EaP). The initiative belonged to Poland and Sweden and aimed to bring the Eastern countries closer to the EU through implementing democratic reforms; the liberalisation of trade and 'gradual integration in the EU economy' (Council of the European Union: 2009); and facilitating travel in the EU for the citizens of these partner countries. The initiative did not offer EU membership perspectives for its members, but aimed to enhance the 'stability, security and prosperity of the European Union and the partner countries and indeed the entire European continent' (Council of the European Union: 2009) through the integration of the six former Soviet republics into the European family of norms and values.

1. The road towards the Eastern Partnership

The EaP was launched within the context of strained EU-Russian relations due to the August 2008 Georgian War and the January 2009 Ukrainian gas crisis. These two events helped accelerate the initiative but they were not its determinants. In fact, the origins of the EaP predate 2004. In April 2002, Great Britain and Denmark proposed a 'New Neighbourhood Initiative', which was initially addressed exclusively to three Eastern European countries; Belarus, Moldova, and Ukraine. The idea of a European initiative for the Eastern neighbours had also been promoted actively by Poland during its preparation for EU membership, between 2002–2004. Warsaw was following Finland's example, which as EU member state advanced the Northern Dimension with the goal of taking the initiative in EU relations with Russia, creating thus its niche within EU foreign policy. In its case, Poland was aspiring to be a civilisational bridge in relations with Belarus, Ukraine, and Moldova, within the Eastern Dimension.

The 2004 accession of ten Central and East European states and the planned membership of Romania and Bulgaria moved the EU's border further towards the East, to three former Soviet republics, Belarus, Moldova, and Ukraine. This brought these three countries to the special attention of Brussels. The 'rose revolution' enhanced the EU's interest in the South Caucasus too, and the May 2004 EU Policy Strategy Paper suggested including Georgia, Armenia, and Azerbaijan, in addition to Belarus, Moldova, and Ukraine, within the scope of the European Neighbourhood Policy (ENP), excluding the Balkans and Turkey from this initiative, given the fact that they had already the status of membership candidate or potential membership candidate.

The Ukrainian 'orange revolution' further enhanced the EU's enthusiasm towards the Eastern neighbourhood, showing that these countries were willing to be part of Europe and needed more attention from Brussels. The events in Ukraine offered also the opportunity to Polish political and diplomatic elites to mediate the political conflict in Kiev, to promote Ukraine's European aspirations, and to label Poland as a true specialist in the Eastern neighbourhood. Along with Warsaw, the other three Visegrád Group countries, the Czech Republic, Slovakia and Hungary; and the Baltic states were some of the most insistent on the necessity of enhancing EU relations with the Eastern neighbours.

The interest towards the new Eastern neighbours was shown also by 'older' EU member states. In 2006, the Austrian Presidency proposed building a joint energy policy, within which Ukraine and Belarus, as transit countries, were to play an important role. The next year, during the German Presidency of the EU, Berlin also expressed its special interest towards the Eastern neighbours. There were even talks about a new *Ostpolitik*, which Germany wanted to translate into an 'ENP Plus' project. However, this initiative was never achieved; Germany changed its priorities in the second part of the EU's mandate, focusing more on Central Asia and the Black

Sea region. Nevertheless, the EaP can be considered as a continuation of discussions that date back to the German Presidency (Cianciara 2009: 25).

The idea of a partnership for the Eastern neighbours took shape with the launch of the Union for the Mediterranean, in 2008. Poland responded actively to France's initiative towards the Southern neighbourhood on the condition that a similar project would be taken into account for the East too, Warsaw highlighting that in the East the EU has European neighbours, while in the South — neighbours of Europe.

The very term 'Eastern Partnership' of the joint Polish-Swedish initiative was used for the first time at the beginning of 2008, during the EU Council. Initially, there was a possibility the project would be launched by Poland and Czech Republic. However, Warsaw preferred to attract an 'older' EU member state, Sweden, in order to avoid the EaP being labelled as an initiative of 'frustrated' Eastern countries. For Swedish foreign minister Carl Bildt, this was a good opportunity to affirm himself as a EU foreign policy specialist and a potential successor of Javier Solana (Ochmann 2009: 4).

The European Council of June 2008 invited the Commission to present a detailed version of this initiative the following spring. However, due to the Georgian war, the Extraordinary European Council convened on 1 September 2008, asked the Commission to present the proposal for the EaP in December 2008. Thus, the Georgian war managed to attract the EU's attention and political will towards the East. Although it did not in itself lead to the EaP, it was a catalyst that speeded up the implementation of the initiative. Moreover, even if the EaP was initially designed only to prevent the moving of the centre of gravity of the ENP towards the South by the launch of the Union for the Mediterranean; the Georgian war and the Ukrainian gas crisis gave it a much greater weight.

Particularly attentive to the developments in the 'near abroad', Moscow did not sympathise with the EaP from the very beginning, looking at it through zero-sum lenses. Russian officials reacted with scepticism to the initiative even before its launch. In March 2009, Russian Foreign Minister, Sergey Lavrov stated that

Brussels wanted to expand its sphere of influence in the area of former Soviet Union through the EaP: 'We are accused of trying to have spheres of influence. What is the 'Eastern Partnership'? Is it a sphere of influence, including Belarus?' And despite Swedish Foreign Minister Carl Bildt's answer that 'the Eastern Partnership is not about spheres of influence. The difference is that these countries themselves opted to join' (Benes 2009), Lavrov did not change his position, insisting on 26 April 2009, in a press conference after the meeting of the EU-Russian Permanent Cooperation Council, that 'We heard statements from Brussels that it's not an attempt to create new zones of influence and not a process directed against Russia. We want to trust these declarations, although some of the EU's comments disquieted us' (Semenij 2010). The Prime-Minister Putin and President Medvedev were even sharper in statements, the first assessed the EaP as 'an alternative to NATO's expansion to the East', while the latter declared that, 'We tried to convince ourselves [that the EaP is not directed against Russia], but in the end, we couldn't. What bothers us is that for some states this is seen as a partnership against Russia' (President of Russia: 2009).

Moscow did not confine itself to statements. That the ceremony of the launching of the EaP, on 7 May 2009, was 'deprived' of shine was due partly to the Kremlin too. It was Russia that succeeded in 'convincing' leaders of some EU and Eastern countries not to attend the event in Prague. The Italian Prime-Minister, Silvio Berlusconi, for instance, had met Russian Prime-Minister, Vladimir Putin less than two weeks before the EaP summit for negotiations on the South Stream gas pipeline and fearing probably not to offend his Russian friend, Berlusconi did not attend the EU summit. Nor did Moldovan President Vladimir Voronin come to Prague. The Moldovan leader had just been congratulated by Moscow on the way he had managed the so-called 'twitter revolution' in Chişinău, and Russia's promise of a $500 million credit line had 'convinced' him that 'This [Eastern Partnership] is similar to the CIS-2. Why should we create another CIS under the control of the EU? It looks like a ring around Russia' (Kommersant 2009). Moldova was represented instead at the EaP summit by the minister of foreign affairs and European integration Andrei Stratan.

2.   Divided or connected by the neighbourhood?

The prosperity and stability of the 'common neighbourhood' is essential for the security of the EU and Russia. Both actors have a huge impact on the 'countries in between'; they both have interests in the neighbourhood and they both are sources of 'carrots and sticks' affecting domestic politics and policies in these states (Casier 2011: 75). However, with different worldviews, Russia and the EU have different approaches towards the 'common neighbourhood'. While the EU manifests a clear interest in stability in these countries and aims at involving them more closely in the European integration process and its trade regime, Russia has a clear interest in keeping the states in this area relatively weak and isolated, in order to maintain its dominance (Casier 2011: 88) and re-create a traditional sphere of influence.

By 'spreading good governance, supporting social and political reform, dealing with corruption and abuse of power, establishing the rule of law and protecting human rights' (The European Security Strategy) in the Eastern partners, the EU provides an authentic democratisation of the region, reinforcing the six states, treating them as independent entities not as pawns organically connected to Russia (Sikorski 2009). Furthermore, through the Eastern Partnership, the EU was demonstrating that the Europeanisation process would not be limited by the 2007 enlargement limits and that the Eastern borders were becoming more porous. '[The EU made] it clear that we are not stopping at the border but we want to enlarge the influence in a democratic way. I mean a way of offering not of putting pressure' (Svoboda 2011). This situation was, however, perceived as a real challenge for the Kremlin, as 'the reorientation of the post-Soviet states towards Europe does not present a threat to the military or economic security of Russia, but it does present a serious modernisation challenge to Moscow' (Kobrinskaya 2007: 20). For example, if Moldova, Ukraine or Georgia adopts EU standards, Russian business in these countries will be forced to become 'EU compatible', creating a growing Russian constituency in favour of Russia adopting EU rules and standards (Vahl 2007: 135). In this way, Chişinău, Kiev or Tbilisi could have an increased role in deepening the linkage between Russia and the West. While a higher linkage to the EU would allow Brussels to increase its leverage towards Russia (see Levitsky and Way 2006).

Within this context, Russia is trying to 'protect' itself by establishing its own version of a 'Monroe doctrine' in the CIS region and 'by establishing a tighter federation highly dependent on the Russian centre but without necessarily expanding Russian territory' (Nygren 2008: 230). The efforts to rebuild a Greater Russia can be seen as expansionist, but not in the traditional geo-political sense of acquiring new territories, but rather of denying others influence (Nygren 2008: 249). It is not the first time that Russia has had such reactions to the EU's influence in an area where the Kremlin has particular interests. The peak of Belarusian-Russian integration, the Union State agreement, was concluded in the same year as the NATO strikes on Serbia that were widely contested both in Russia and Belarus (Verpoest 2007: 164).

However, Russia's policy based on 'spheres of influence' is not only in opposition to EU's policies in the 'common neighbourhood' but is contesting also the EU-Russia Common Space of External Security (Avere 2009: 1702). Brussels rejects the idea of a Russian 'privileged sphere of interests' in the region, as the EU considers that Russia has to accept that the countries of the shared neighbourhood have the right to choose their own way and foreign policy. The EU seeks a European 'postmodern' security community across the wider Europe and the creation of a 'ring of well governed countries' to the East (Avere 2009: 1690) and is implementing this through 'soft and smart power', projecting security and creating prosperity. The EU strives for the harmonisation of states' legal systems with the EU's *acquis communautaire* and for the creation of suitable conditions for political integration through shared values (Tumanov 2011: 130). These are the aims of the EaP.

3.   Is the EaP a challenge for Russian foreign policy?

The EaP aims to transform the partner countries into democratic, prosperous and stable neighbours, a situation which would benefit both the EU and Russia at least in terms of border security. However, while the EU perceives the EaP as a win-win situation, for the Kremlin, still trapped in a realist way of thinking in matters of foreign policy, the initiative appears as a challenge to its interests in the 'near abroad'. President Medvedev clearly stated after the Georgian War that 'Russia, like other countries in the world, has regions where it has privileged interests, [and that] these are regions where countries with which we have friendly relations are located', or, in other words, that the Kremlin has special interests in the former Soviet republics and intrusions by others into these regions that undermine pro-Russian regimes will be regarded as a threat to Russia's 'special interests' (Friedman 2008). Within this context, we can notice that from a Russian point of view, the EaP is not seen as a selfless European initiative to help the former Soviet republics, but as the EU's attempt to deprive Moscow of its 'spheres of influence'.

As the challenges that the former Soviet republics have been dealing with are mainly internal: feeble governance, weak institutions, fragile civil society, and runaway corruption, Russia merely ignores the inner weaknesses of these states, while promoting her own strategic interests. However, the EaP aims to tackle these issues and to provide an authentic democratisation of the region, reinforcing the six states, treating them as independent entities not as pawns organically connected to Russia (Sikorski 2009). The guidelines might prove real geo-political challenges for Russia. If achieved, Moscow would find it difficult to influence the political class and the resolutions of the former Soviet republics and, thus, would be unable to claim supremacy over the CIS space.

Until the launch of the EaP, Moscow saw the EU as a relatively benign international organisation, a strategic ally in a desired multipolar world. More concerned with the USA's foreign policy, Russia saw the EU enlargement as a fairly positive process, which would have provided a convenient alternative to NATO's expansion (Karabeshkin and Spechler 2007: 308). Thus, while the Kremlin saw an American hand in what happened in the 'near abroad' after 2000, reading the 'colour revolutions' as largely U.S. conspiratorial activities meant to drastically reduce Russia's influence in the neighbourhood, and expand the United States' (Trenin 2009: 12);

with no accession prospects and comprising a too large an area, the launch of the ENP was seen in Moscow rather as an attempt to establish a buffer zone around the EU, a convenient '*cordon sanitaire* for the Kremlin.

With the EaP, however, Moscow's attitude towards Brussels underwent a major change. The initiative made Russia much more worried about the EU. The speed with which the 27 EU members mobilised to launch the EaP and the strengthening of the EU after the entry into force of the Treaty of Lisbon, changed Russia's thinking. For Moscow, the EU became the major rival in the 'near abroad', especially given that 'the EU is the only great power with unsettled borders' (Krastev 2005).

A modern international actor, for Russia, the idea of sovereignty is at the centre of its view of itself, its neighbours and the state system in Europe. The very existence of the post-modern EU is based, however, on the ceding by its member states of parts of their sovereignty to the supranational organisation. On the other side, the EU's philosophy supports the principle that democratic countries are least likely to engage in wars with other democratic states, as long as they respect fundamental rules and human rights. However, these facts lead to limitations of sovereignty of a state because the international laws restrict the authority of governments to act over their own territory. Russia still perceives the principle of sovereignty in Westphalian terms where the national government has complete control within its borders and a complete monopoly on power. Therefore, from Moscow's point of view, the EU's policy for supporting respect for human rights and promotion of democratic values in the EaP countries is seen not as well-intended attempts to ensure the stability and security of the European continent but as unacceptable interference in the domestic affairs of the former Soviet republics and thus in its 'sphere of influence' (Haukkala 2010, 103).

The EU's external governance especially when it involves institutionalised frameworks for political dialogue (i.e. the EaP), networks or non-state actors (i.e. Civil Society Forum), contrasts with Russia's traditional politics of power (Dimitrova and Dragneva

2010: 63). The notion of governance presupposes forms of organisation that go beyond hard notions of external and internal sovereignty (Lavenex 2004: 682). Through the EaP, the EU's external governance penetrates in fact the spheres of domestic policy of non-member states, transferring parts of the *acquis communautaire* and making the borders with Eastern neighbours more fluid and porous. This fact is seen by Russia as a real challenge to its foreign policy goals in the six former Soviet republics, the Kremlin perceiving the EU's export of parts of the *acquis communautaire* as an intrusion into its sphere of influence.

Given these differences in worldviews, we can explain why the Kremlin perceives the EaP as a challenge for its foreign policy and why Russia attempts to constrain the EU's external policy in the EaP countries. Thus, by using economic pressure, alternative integrationist projects, and commitments in the CIS framework, the Kremlin seeks in fact to compete with the EU in exporting policies and rules.

It is not difficult to notice that Russia's integrationist projects experienced a revival after the launch of the EaP. The Customs Union was implemented in 2010, Putin's 'soul project', the Eurasian Union was announced unexpectedly less than a week after the second Eastern Partnership summit, on 3 October 2011, while two weeks later, Russia, Ukraine, Moldova, Belarus, Armenia, Kazakhstan, Kyrgyzstan and Tajikistan signed an agreement for creating a free trade zone within the framework of the CIS. On the eve of a 2013 EaP summit in Vilnius, after a visit to Moscow, the president of Armenia, one of the possible candidates for signing an Association Agreement with the EU, announced abruptly that his country would join the Russia-led Customs Union, becoming thus incompatible with the provisions of the EU's Deep and Comprehensive Free Trade Agreement. Finally, on 1st January 2015 was launched the Eurasian Economic Union and on 2nd January, Armenia joined it.

It is clear that Russia is trying to counteract the EU's initiative by offering alternatives to the former Soviet republics. However, the Kremlin traditionally understands only a paternalist type of integration, an integration that presupposes preferential treatment in exchange for following Moscow's policy (Kobrinskaya 2007: 20). In other words, Russia recognises the independence of the former Soviet republics, but it does not mean implicitly that it is ready to respect their sovereignty too. While the EU endeavours to ensure its own security and stability by supporting the EaP countries and integrating them in a community of common values, Russia's interest is to keep the former Soviet republics relatively weak and isolated, in order to maintain its dominance. The Kremlin is trying to maintain or re-create a traditional sphere of influence that gives Moscow a *droit de regard* over its former possessions. A 'liberal empire', with the strategic tasks of re-engaging Russia as the economic and cultural 'natural and unique leader' of the CIS seems to be close to the Russian approach towards former Soviet republics.

Russia is afraid of losing influence in the former Soviet territories and perceives the Eastern Partnership as a challenge to its foreign policy goals. In fact, Russia is still trapped in the old ways of thinking, perceiving the West as a threat (Barysch 2011: 14). The traditional approach of Russian security thinking reflects Russia's fears that the country is encircled by enemies and, thus, that it needs to seek allies and create buffer zones or a 'liberal empire' against dangers (Haas 2009: 4). Within this context, we can understand why the Kremlin perceived this European initiative as a real challenge to its traditional realist foreign policy and why it tries to bind the former Soviet republics into alternative concurrent integrationist projects (e.g. Eurasian Economic Union).

Conclusions

Even if the first impulse of an uninstructed public would be to link the EaP with the 2008 Georgian War, implying that the European initiative came as a reaction to Moscow's military actions in the Caucasian neighbouring country, the data show that the demarches for the EaP started before August 2008. Indeed, the Russo-Georgian war propelled the Polish-Swedish initiative, however, it did not determine its inception. Within this context, a zero-sum approach of the EaP appears inappropriate.

The EaP aims to help the six former Soviet republics to strengthen their institutions, and develop their economy, to no one's detriment. It gives the six partner countries access to the largest market in the world and aims to enhance their energy security. All of these elements, once achieved, could make the six former Soviet republics more stable and more independent, which should be a win-win situation both for Brussels and Moscow than need security and prosperity at their borders.

Although the EaP aims to be a win-win initiative it was not received well at all by the Kremlin and had a strong impact on Moscow's perceptions of the EU. If before the EaP Moscow's main concern in the 'near abroad' was NATO extension, the Polish-Swedish initiative made Russia see a new competitor for influence in the CIS area. After the launch of the EaP, Russia has been increasingly wary of European initiatives that endanger its generally dominant political, cultural and economic position in the region (Lukyanov 2008b). Russia started to see the EU, for the first time, as a competitor for influence in the former Soviet republics (Umland 2011b), and as a threat to its foreign policy based on realist principles of spheres of influence. If the 2004 and 2007 EU enlargements were disturbing, at least there was established a clear borderline, while the European Neighbourhood Policy (ENP) was perceived more as an initiative to establish a *cordon sanitaire* between the EU and the 'others'. With the EaP, however, the Kremlin perceived the EU as a real challenger to its interests in the former Soviet republics. Through its power of attraction and external incentives aimed at 'creating the necessary conditions to accelerate political association and further economic integration between the European Union and interested partner countries' (Council of the European Union 2009) the EaP made it clear that the EU is not stopping at the border but wants to enlarge its influence in a democratic way, a way of offering incentives, not of bringing pressure to bear (Swoboda 2011). Through its policies, the EaP made the borders between the EU and the six former Soviet republics more porous, allowing the Europeanisation process to expand outside the EU and transferring parts of the *acquis communautaire* to its Eastern neighbours.

Chapter 5
Russia's Contribution to the Inception of the EaP

Introduction

Although the EaP was initiated by the Polish and Swedish foreign ministers and highlights the need to bring the Eastern neighbours closer to Europe for the EU's own security and stability, the initiative was not conceived only for the European Union's sake. The Eastern partners joined the EaP voluntarily. They opted to commit themselves to a series of costly reforms not because they were pressed by Brussels but because they were aware that those efforts would bring not only long term economic advantages but also the preservation and enhancement of their sovereignty. As we argue below, the short history of the foreign policy of the former Soviet republics shows that, despite Russian pressure, these countries have been trying to approach the EU instead of the Kremlin, both for the need of protecting their regimes' core values and because of their will to (re)construct their European identity. Thus, the EaP came to meet the wills and needs of both the EU and the Eastern neighbours.

1. The first signs of disobedience in the 'near abroad'

The former Soviet republics are one of the priorities of Moscow's foreign policy. The 'near abroad' is seen both paramount for Russia's security and for its international prestige vis-à-vis the other poles of the multipolar international system. The interest towards these countries was clearly stated by every foreign policy concept of the Russian Federation. Even the term 'near abroad' (ближнее зарубежье) used in Russian diplomatic jargon with reference to the former Soviet republics, proves a special status 'granted' to them. It may imply that these countries are not as foreign as others and therefore should be subject to different rules or treatment, or that

Russia has 'special rights' and responsibilities for maintaining security within this region (Aydin and Kaptanolu 2008: 764). The January 1994 speech of the Russian foreign minister Kozyrev at the
conference with Baltic and CIS ambassadors supports this idea. In
the speech, Kozyrev claimed that 'the CIS and the Baltic states con-
stitutes the area in which Russia's principal vital interests are concentrated ... [and] from which the main threats to its interest ema-
nate. We should not withdraw from these regions which have been
in the sphere of Russian interests for centuries' (Arbatov1997: 429).

In general, Russia's special interest in the 'near abroad' results
from economic factors, diaspora issues and, more importantly,
from its own security needs. Embedded in a realist worldview, obsessed by a fear of being encircled by enemies, Moscow perceives
the former Soviet republics to be paramount for the protection of its
own borders. Thus, as throughout history, Belarus proved to be the
land through which the Western invaders made their way towards
central Russia and Moscow, the Kremlin tries to keep this country
as close as possible as a precaution. Ukraine is seen as the south-
western anchor and Russia's Achilles' heel. Moldova is for Ukraine
what Ukraine is to Russia, therefore, if Ukraine cannot be defended,
Russia cannot either (Friedman 2010a), the smallest former Soviet
republic 'earning' thus a strategic importance for Russia; while the
Transcaucasus or the South Caucasus (Georgia, Armenia and Azerbaijan) is a buffer zone and an area of rivalry between Russia, Turkey, Iran and the USA. For the purpose of this book, we will refer
only to these six former Soviet republics as forming the 'near
abroad'.

With the 2004–2007 EU enlargement, Russia's 'near abroad'
also became the EU's neighbourhood. However, this reality is apparently not very comfortable for the Kremlin, suspicious that in
the balance of power logic, the EU would strengthen its positions
to Russia's detriment. Haukkala (2010: 137) argues that even the
syntagm 'common neighbourhood', proposed by the EU in official
documents bothered Russian authorities because it could have
hinted at some challenge to its sphere of influence, Moscow preferring instead the expression 'countries adjacent to Russia' and 'countries adjacent to the EU'.

The 'near abroad' is at the core of Russian foreign policy (Prystayko 2008: 59) and the intensive links created during a three-four generations common history and strong economic leverage gives Moscow an advantageous position in relations with these states. Within this context one can presume that the Kremlin's task to 'keep the EU at distance' from the former Soviet republics while having friendly relations with these countries should not encounter many difficulties. Yet, the Eastern partners have contradicted this scenario from the very beginning of their independence.

Before the disintegration of the USSR many intellectuals and Russian policy-makers were arguing that should Russia get rid of the other Soviet republics, its people's standard of living was likely to elevate to that of Japan and Germany (Fakiolas and Fakiolas 2004: 388). Thus, on the one hand it appeared that, alone, Russia would not have to subsidise other republics and would get rid of a financial burden, allowing the country to integrate quickly into the Western economic community, and, on the other hand, the Kremlin was eager to get rid of a neo-imperialist image from its foreign policy, arguing that an imperialist Russia could not be at the same time a democratic country (Aydin and Kaptanolu 2008: 765). Within this context, at its inception, the CIS was planned as an organisation designed to make an easy 'civilised divorce' of the former Soviet republics, this thinking fitting the liberal internationalism paradigm — dominant in Russia's foreign policy at that time.

However, this liberal approach towards the former Soviet republics together with the apparent Russia's 'Western honeymoon' did not last too long. The parliamentary elections of December 1993 represented a defeat of the liberal reformers and a shift of Russian foreign policy to more traditional realist concepts, promoted by the great power balancers (Kuchins and Zevelev 2012: 153). The regret about lost influence in international politics translated quickly into a policy of keeping the former Soviet republics, except for the Baltics, within the Russian sphere of influence (Rywkin 2003: 4). The 'near abroad' was seen indispensable for the Kremlin to maintain the great power status. As according to the realist worldview only powers that are important centres of gravity are subjects and not objects of international order. The interest for the 'near abroad' was officially proclaimed by the 14 September 1995 presidential decree, 'The strategic course of the Russian Federation with the CIS states', that asserted the need to 'intensify integration within the CIS and to improve coordination of Russian executive bodies' activities in this direction' (Brzezinski and Sullivan 1997: 201). This interest was later established also by the National Security Concept of the Russian Federation, approved by President Yeltsin in December 1997. The document specifies that cooperation within the CIS was a priority of Russian foreign policy and the 'deepening and development of relations with the CIS countries is the most important factor' (Концепция национальной безопасности Российской Федерации 1997). The replacement, in January 1996, of Andrei Kozyrev by Yevgenii Primakov as Foreign Minister only confirmed the shift in Russian diplomacy from a liberal internationalism to a great power balancing paradigm, accompanied by Moscow's desire to establish its diplomatic and security hegemony throughout the territory of the former Soviet Union (Lynch 2002: 166).

However, Russia's position in the 'near abroad' was far from making its hegemonic policy an easy task. Among the former Soviet republics of the 'common neighbourhood', Russia had cordial relations in that period only with Armenia and Belarus, with the latter forming a union state since 1996. Moldova, Georgia and Azerbaijan were attempting to promote radical Westernising orientations, in the manner of the three Baltic States with their independence. Unfortunately, these states failed and 'got' instead civil wars and a loss of central control over separatist enclaves (Kuzio 2000: 82). All three countries have reluctantly become CIS members: fearing economic blockade and hoping to solve a separatist conflict. Moldova signed an agreement to join the CIS in 1991, however, the parliament ratified it only in April 1994. Azerbaijan withdrew from the CIS in October 1992 and turned to Turkey for assistance in the Nagorno-Karabakh conflict, even signing a deal to build a new oil pipeline from Baku to the Turkish port of Ceyhan. However, the coup of June 1993, where many saw Russia's fingerprints (Kubicek 2000: 562), brought Heidar Aliev to power, a former Politburo member, who, in gratitude, rejoined the CIS in September 1993 and suspended talks with Western companies on oil and pipeline development. Having decided to remain outside the CIS, Georgia was also obliged to join the Russian-led organisation in 1993 (Bakshi 2000: 1272). In the context of intensified fighting in Abkhazia and the resurgence of Gamsakhurdia forces in western Georgia (in both cases a Russian hand being obviously seen (Kubicek 2000: 563)) and internationally isolated, Tbilisi joined the CIS and gave Russia five bases on its territory, in exchange for brokering peace with Abkhazia and help against Gamsakhurdia.

Even the second biggest Slavic republic tried to consolidate its independence from Russia and restricted its involvement within the CIS to a 'fake participation'. Ukraine did not withdraw from the organisation, fearing territorial losses (President Yeltsin clearly stated that Russia would recognise Ukraine's borders only within the CIS borders), however, the parliament has not ratified the CIS Charter, and, thus Kiev is not *de jure* a CIS member, its involvement in the organisation being defined as a 'participant' (Kuzio 2000: 84). Furthermore, Ukraine had tried to establish an anti-Russian *cordon sanitaire* in 1993 under the label of a Baltic-Black Sea alliance of states lying between Russia and Germany (Kuzio 2000: 89), and later became the catalyst of GUAM.

The unsuccessful military campaign in Chechnya in 1994–1996 showed Russia's weakness and encouraged the countries from the 'near abroad' to distance themselves again from Moscow. Azerbaijan fostered multinational companies to invest in its energy resources in order to eliminate its economic dependency on Russia; Georgia was repeatedly accusing Russian peace-keepers of siding with Abkhazian separatists (Fakiolas and Fakiolas 2004: 388); Moldova was striving to approach the EU; while Ukraine was backing NATO expansion and upgraded relations with NATO to a special partnership (Kubicek 2000: 561). In 1997, these countries established, in Strasbourg, GUAM (Georgia, Ukraine, Azerbaijan and Moldova), an organisation that pursues integration into transatlantic and European structures to try to diminish the dependence of its members on Russia (Rywkin 2003: 8). The four former Soviet republics were seeking also to deprive the right of the CIS to represent them in international organisations, to prevent the use of economic levers by Russia, to obtain strategic concessions through the CIS, and were opposing the right of the CIS to resolve armed conflicts within the CIS (Kuzio 2000: 94), Georgia and Azerbaijan looking instead to the USA to help them solve the protracted internal conflicts. The anti-Russian orientation of GUAM was confirmed by the attendance of its members at the 50th anniversary NATO summit in Washington in April 1999, during NATO's bombardment in Serbia, where Uzbekistan joined the organisation, transforming the acronym in GUUAM.

The inception of GUAM/GUUAM was proving that Russia was steadily losing influence in the former Soviet republics. The agreement on the Baku Ceyhan pipeline in November 1999 confirmed this assessment. Primakov stated on several occasions that great power status did not come cheaply and that Russia should pay the economic price for reintegrating the old empire, directly or indirectly (Lynch 2002: 167). However, the Kremlin did not have the necessary economic and military capabilities for achieving its declared goals of consolidating Russia's positions in the 'near abroad'.

2.   Towards an assertive approach

When Vladimir Putin came to power in December 1999, Russian foreign policy was in disarray. The relations with the West had deteriorated after the Kosovo war, while the ties with Russia's neighbours had atrophied (Stent 2008: 1090). In one of his first public speeches, the new president announced that the relations with the CIS members would be a priority for him, making clear that the former Soviet republics were of great geopolitical and geostrategic importance for the Kremlin. The interest towards the 'near abroad' was also recorded by the National Security Concept of the Russian Federation, adopted on January 10, 2000. The document states the development of Russia's relations with the CIS members in accordance with 'principles of international law' and in the manner 'of meeting Russia's interests' (Концепция национальной безопасности Российской Федерации 2000).

The new president took a much more pragmatic attitude towards the 'near abroad' than his predecessor. Putin made it clear that the CIS was not going to be anymore a 'posthumous version of the Soviet Union, a 'politburo of equals' with the leaders of the now independent republics seemingly enjoying equality with the Moscow boss' (Trenin 2009: 9), that the former Soviet republics have to comply with Russia's security parameters and 'they can no longer expect concessional treatment as with 'buddy Yeltsin' and get away with it' (Bakshi 2000: 1283), they had to meet 'Russia's interests'. This trend was reinforced a year later by the then Secretary of the Security Council, Sergei Ivanov, when he publicly acknowledged that previous attempts to integrate the CIS had come at a very high price, and that Russia must now abandon the integration project in favour of a 'pragmatic' course of bilateral relations. It has to be noticed that at that moment CIS states' debt to Russia had reached $5.5 billion (Tsygankov 2006: 1082).

Putin's determination in its policy towards the CIS was enhanced by a combination of internal and external factors. Rising oil prices helped Russia to recover quickly from the economic crisis, victory over the Chechen insurgency restored confidence in country's might, the centralisation of power and the defeat of oligarchs stabilised the country, while the closeness between Russia and the USA after 11 September 2001 made Putin assume that in return for supporting the American anti-terrorist campaign Washington would recognise Russia's sphere of influence in the 'near abroad', as long as, from the Kremlin's perspective it is natural that great powers have special influence in their neighbourhood, as the USA does in Latin America (Stent 2008: 1095).

Thus, having economic power and internationally consolidated positions, Putin's Russia took a more decisive and stronger attitude in its relations with the former Soviet republics. The Kremlin put pressure on Georgia to allow Russian troops to pursue Chechen rebels into its territory; Moscow resisted withdrawing its forces from Moldova and Georgia, as it had promised at the OSCE's 1999 conference; put pressure on GUUAM and tried to 'convince' Azerbaijan to give up the idea of construction of Baku-Ceyhan pipeline (Rywkin 2003: 9). Putin showed also his readiness to play the diaspora card in Moldova and Ukraine to justify his efforts to gain influence. In June 2000, the Russian president declared that 'Russia is interested in Moldova being a territorially whole, independent state. But this cannot be achieved unless the interests of all population groups, including [the] Transdniester population, are observed' (Blank 2002: 155). Furthermore, the threat of secessionism was enforced by the December 17, 2001, constitutional law, 'On the procedure for the admittance/acceptance to the Russian Federation and the founding within its framework of a New Subject of the Russian federation' – a clear warning for the former Soviet republics that Moscow could decide to 'admit' Abkhazia, South Ossetia, Transnistria, or some other regions within its own borders (Kurdiukov and Malfliet 2007: 208).

In addition, where it was possible, Vladimir Putin has tried to replace pro-Western politicians in the CIS countries with pro-Moscow figures. Moscow pressured Kiev to fire its foreign minister Tarasyuk, in November 2000 and its prime-minister Yushchenko, in May 2001 and appointed the former chairman of Gazprom and former Russian prime-minister, Viktor Chernomyrdin, ambassador to Kiev with the aim of taking advantage of Ukraine's main economic weakness – the dependence on Russian energy (Rywkin 2003: 9). The FSB, the Russian intelligence service, has also helped Ukrainian police arrest the former energy minister and opposition leader Iulia Tymoshenko, in February 2001, on the basis of five-year-old bribery charges (Blank 2002: 154). Within this context of Russia's intrusion in the domestic policies of the 'near abroad', we can assume that Moscow must have also had a 'contribution' in the discrediting of Chişinău's pro-European Sturza Government and in the victory of the pro-Russian Party of Communists of the Republic of Moldova in the 2001 parliamentary elections.

These examples are a clear reflection of the fact that Russia did not regard the former Soviet republics as fully-fledged independent states to be dealt with on an equal basis but as 'subjects' of its sphere of influence (Rywkin 2003: 4). They are too small to 'have the right' to take part in the decisions in world affairs, being condemned to gravitate around the sovereign pole, Russia. The project of a liberal empire, announced by Anatoly Chubais in 2003, appeared only to support Moscow's (neo)realist worldview. The former head of Russia's privatisation presented the liberal empire as the only viable project for securing market and democratic reforms in the CIS, assuming that the West would endorse it. In Chubais' opinion, in return for a free market and a stable Russia and surrounding region, the West would have to recognise Russia's sphere of influence (Chubais 2003). And even if the 'colour revolutions' prevented the building of the liberal empire, elements of this project, like 'promotion of the expansion of domestic business in the neighbouring countries both in trade and in the acquisition and development of assets' (Chubais 2003), left their mark on Moscow's policy towards the 'near abroad'.

The 'rose revolution' in Georgia and the 'orange revolution' in Ukraine that led to the defeat of pro-Russian leaders in Tbilisi and Kiev came as a real political earthquake for Moscow. The most dramatic failure was perceived in Ukraine, where the Kremlin poured substantial resources into supporting Yanukovich, President Kuchama's designated heir (Stent 2008: 1100). For Putin, such behaviour of the 'near abroad' was unacceptable. Even if, to a great extent, it was the Kremlin's actions in the 'near abroad' that triggered the 'colour revolutions': Russian pressure and interference in the political process of these neighbours brought people into the streets, determined to defend the sovereignty of their country, to break with their recent past and to engage in an effective reform process that would enable their rapprochement with the West; for Moscow it was the West that 'set' the 'colour revolutions'. Thus, instead of revising its foreign policy towards the former Soviet republics in the sense of rapprochement of these countries to the Kremlin, by treating them as equal sovereign states and establishing relationships based on confidence and international democratic rules, Moscow's actions in the 'near abroad' after 2004–2005 have done nothing but further alienated these countries.

Aware of the strategic importance of the 'near abroad', especially for the export of oil and gas — the key of Russia's great-powerness revival, Moscow sought to secure its rising revenues and strengthen its positions in the neighbouring republics so as to prevent any new 'West orchestrated colour uprisings'. What followed was labelled by many scholars as the *economisation* of Russian foreign policy, translated into increasing the gas price for the former Soviet republics, acquisition of strategic infrastructure of these states through assets-for-debt agreements, trade blackmail, and deportation of illegal workers; and a more active use of protracted separatist conflicts in the 'near abroad' in order to put more pressure on the central 'disobedient' governments.

2.1. The 'energodiplomacy'

What the USSR sought to achieve with nuclear weapons, Russia under Putin was trying to achieve with oil and gas — increased political influence over its neighbours and the EU (Stent 2008: 1094). The clearest example in this sense is the 'gas offensive' on the 'near abroad' that followed the 'colour revolutions'. In fact, the idea of using energy weapons for influencing the post-Soviet countries, which we labelled as 'energodiplomacy', did not appear after the popular revolts in Georgia and Ukraine. It had already been developed by the doctrine of Liberal Empire but has been implemented in all countries analysed in the present book immediately after the democratic revolutions in the 'near abroad'.

Shortly after Yushchenko was installed as president in Kiev, Russia, through the state-owned Gazprom, demanded a sharp increase in price for gas exported to Ukraine, from $50 per thousand cubic meters (tcm) to $160 per tcm and then to $230 per tcm, arguing the necessity of adjustment to the current market price. Kiev resisted, stating that an existing agreement guaranteed a low price until 2009 (Nichol, Woehrel, Gelb 2006: 2). Consequently, on 31 December 2005, Gazprom cut off natural gas supplies to Ukraine, which made Kiev divert some gas transiting the country to European customers for its own use. After European governments' protests, Gazprom resumed gas deliveries on January 2, and two days later a preliminary agreement between Gazprom and Ukraine was reached. In 2007, the two parties agreed to gradually increase the price of Russian gas supplied to Ukraine over the next five years, until it reached the world market price (Woehrel 2009: 8). However, the frictions resumed shortly afterwards. After the narrow victory of pro-Western parties in the Ukrainian September 2007 parliamentary elections, Gazprom suddenly asked Ukraine to pay its $ 1.3 billion gas debts in less than a month. In March 2008 Gazprom reduced gas supplies by 50% because of the disagreement on the price Ukraine should have paid for gas delivered in January and February 2008, the supplies being restored after two days. While on January 1, 2009, Russia stopped gas supplies to Ukraine, and on January 6 – all deliveries through Ukraine to the rest of Europe, causing the worst gas crisis up to that point. It was only on January 18 that Russia and Ukraine reached an agreement and gas supplies to Europe were resumed on January 20, after 13 days of cold winter.

The Republic of Moldova was also affected by the 2005–2006 Russian 'gas offensive'. At the end of 2005, Gazprom announced to Moldovan authorities that it intended to double the price of natural gas. As Chişinău opposed this, on January 1, 2006, Gazprom halted natural gas supplies to Moldova. The crisis lasted until mid-January, when the two sides agreed to increase the price for Moldovan recipients from $80 per tcm to $110 per tcm, after which it rose to $160 per tcm, explained by some specialists as a 'coercion' for Chişinău's pro-Western policy (Gromadzki and Kononczuk 2007: 22). In December 2006, the two sides reached an agreement, which provided that Moldova would pay $170 per tcm in 2007 and the price would gradually increase up to $250 per tcm in 2011. In addition, Gazprom received 13% of Transnistria's stake in MoldovaGaz, increasing thus the percentage of its shares in Moldova's owner of natural gas pipelines to 63.4%.

Much the same pattern followed the gas dispute in Georgia in 2006. At the end of 2005 Gazprom announced to Tbilisi its intention to substantially increase the price of gas. In January 2006, unknown saboteurs bombed the Tbilisi-Mozdok pipeline in North Ossetia, stopping temporarily gas supplies to Georgia. The incident coincided with an explosion on an electricity supply line near the Georgian border and was labelled as a deliberate act of sabotage by Georgian President Saakashvilli who insinuated a link between the explosions and the dispute over gas prices (BBC 2006a). In November 2006, Gazprom threatened Tbilisi that it would cut off gas supplies by the end of the year if Georgia did not agree to an increased price or sold its main gas pipeline to Gazprom (Woehrel 2009: 11). However, in mid-2006, the Baku-Tbilisi-Ceyhan oil pipeline was completed, and in March 2007, the South Caucasus gas pipeline (Baku-Tbilisi-Erzurum) started transporting gas from Azerbaijan to Turkey via Georgia, allowing Tbilisi to lessen its dependence on Russia.

Gazprom's attempts to impose higher prices on Azerbaijan made Baku decide not to import natural gas from Russia anymore. In addition, the State Oil Company of the Azerbaijani Republic (SOCAR) halted on January 1, 2007, its oil exports to Russia via the Baku-Novorossiisk pipeline for three months, arguing that the oil was needed to be used as fuel for Azerbaijani power stations that used to run on Russian gas (Blagov 2007).

Neither have the 'friendly' neighbours escaped Russian gas pressure. In January 2006, Armenia was informed by Gazprom of its intentions to double the price of Russian gas, from $56 per tcm to $110 per tcm. Depending totally on Russian supplies, in May, the country ceded various energy assets to Russian firms as partial payment for this price increase and in October the same year, Armenian officials announced that Gazprom would assume management control of the Iranian-Armenian gas pipeline, then under construction.

The last neighbour encountering Russian 'economisation' of foreign policy was Belarus. A member of the state union, the most loyal to Moscow among former Soviet republics, Belarus used to receive natural gas at Russia's domestic prices. However, in April 2006, the deputy CEO of Gazprom declared that the rate of natural gas supplied to Belarus 'should be at least three times higher' (Ria-Novosti 2006), meaning around $140 per tcm. Belarus was threatened with a cut off in supplies on January 1, 2007, if did not agree to pay the higher price. The gas shutoff was prevented by an agreement reached just hours before the deadline, on December 31, 2006. Belarus accepted an increase in the price of gas from $46,68 per tcm to $100 per tcm and a gradual adjustment, reaching world market levels in 2011. Additionally, Belarus agreed to sell Gazprom 50 percent of the stock in Beltransgaz, the Belarusian gas pipeline company (Aleksandrov 2007: 12).

However, the conflict between the two countries erupted again a week later over the price of oil. The dispute was started by Moscow's decision to impose a duty of $180 per ton on oil exports to Belarus. In response, Minsk decided to increase the custom duties on the transport of Russian oil through Belarus to $45 per ton. Russia stopped pumping oil to Europe via the Druzba pipeline, which crosses Belarus, accusing its neighbour of siphoning off oil. After negotiations, Belarus cancelled its customs duties on oil, while Russia reduced the export customs for oil delivered to Belarus from $180 to $53 per tcm.

The *asset-for-debt strategy* also fits the context of 'energodiplomacy'. Initiated during Putin's first term, this policy consists of forcing indebted CIS countries to cede to Russia their strategic assets in exchange for debts. At the beginning, it was the electricity production and distribution of countries in the 'near abroad' that were affected. Through this strategy, the Russian Unified Energy Systems (UES), headed by Anatoly Chubais, the author of the liberal empire concept, acquired a 75% share in a Georgian electricity distribution company, obtained the right to manage several power plants and owned 50% of the Transenergy nuclear power plant and all of the Mitkvari power plant. In Armenia, UES came to control 100% of the country's electricity production and distribution (Nygren 2008: 244).

As it has been noticed above, the policy of assets-for-debt was used more effectively during the 2005–2006 gas offensive. With strong energy leverage during the cold winter, Moscow has succeeded in increasing its stake in Moldova's pipeline system, bought the main Georgian gas pipeline, took control of the construction of the Iranian-Armenian pipeline and received half of the stock in a Belarusian pipeline company. In November 2011, Russia took control of the entire Belarusian pipeline system.

These actions have strengthened Russia's economic positions in the 'near abroad' allowing Moscow to put more pressure on the governments of the former Soviet republics; however, the gas wars and the acquisition of strategic assets have disappointed the ordinary people from these countries, providing the necessary public support to their political leaders in the decision to reorient their foreign policy towards the West.

2.2. From 'food wars' to deportations

Within the context of the *economisation* of Russian foreign policy the 'food wars' with the former Soviet republics played an important role too. Aiming to put pressure on its neighbours, the Kremlin did not hesitate to hit on the main exports of these countries. For this purpose the imposition of periodic trade embargos and other economic sanctions on countries dependent on Russian market are a strong source of political pressure (Bugajski 2010: 13).

Still affected by the gas wars, in March 2006, Russia put an import ban on both Moldovan and Georgian wines, on the grounds that they contained dangerous substances, in particular pesticides and hard metals, and that many drinks were falsified. At that moment, the Russian market accounted for between 80–90% of Moldova's and Georgia's total wine exports (BBC 2006b). Five weeks later, Russia banned another of Georgia's prominent exports – Borjomi and Nabeglavi mineral water, alleging that the products failed to meet water purity standards. These embargoes came within the context of Georgia's efforts to join NATO and Moldova's pro-Western orientation. Furthermore, Putin had apparently inserted the wine trade as an issue in the negotiations with Moldova on the Transnistrian conflict (Socor 2007). In late 2007, amid the warming of relations between Chișinău and Moscow, Russia lifted the ban on Moldovan wine; the embargo on Georgian products remained in force, however.

Also, in 2006, Russia boycotted Belarusian sugar, accusing Minsk of 'dumping' by exporting cheap sugar made from imported Cuban sugar cane, arguing that the agreements with Russia on Belarusian sugar exports applied only to sugar made of local beets (Belarus Digest 2012). The dispute ended in 2007, when Belarus agreed to cut its exports of sugar to the Russian market.

That Russian 'food wars' had a punitive character and only apparent consumer protection aims has been further proven also by the subsequent forms. One month after the launch of the EaP, Russia imposed a ban on Belarusian milk and dairy products, citing Belarus' failure to meet new Russian sanitary regulations. In August 2010, a new ban was introduced on imports of Moldovan wine, ahead of parliamentary elections, planned in autumn; in February 2012, Ukrainian cheese was banned from the Russian market on the basis that it contained palm oil; in March 2012, Russia threatened to restrict Azerbaijani exports of fruits and vegetables, in the context of negotiations of a Russian radar station on its territory; while in July 2013, the Kremlin chief sanitary officials banned imports of a popular Ukrainian chocolate brand, within the context of Kiev's 'stubbornness' in refusing Customs Union membership, while looking instead for an Association Agreement with the EU.

In the logic of economic wars fits as well the 2006 deportation of Georgians from Russia. In retaliation for the arrest by Georgian authorities of four Russian citizens on charges of espionage in September 2006, the Kremlin suspended transport and communication links to Georgia and stopped issuing visas to Georgian citizens, aiming to prevent Georgian migrant workers in Russia from sending money back home. This decision was shortly followed by a campaign of expelling Georgians who were in Russia illegally and discrediting those who remained, the anti-Georgian media campaign provoking discriminatory actions against Georgian owners of food and entertainment venues in Russian cities. There was little doubt that these sanctions were intended to encourage Georgian people to bring down Saakashvilli (Ducan 2012: 15). Given the fact that at that time it was estimated that more than a fifth of Georgia's 4.4 million people (almost 1 million) were working in Russia (International Herald Tribune 2006), and their remittances sent home reached $1 billion annually, representing 20–25% of Georgia's GDP (Tsygankov 2006: 1092), Russia's actions could not be interpreted only as attempts to destabilise Georgia.

2.3. The secessionist card

As one can notice, the Russian offensive towards the former Soviet republics became more assertive, better coordinated and more quickly triggered after the 'colour revolutions'. This trend was already hinted in April 2005, when President Putin addressed the Russian nation, saying that the demise of the Soviet Union was the greatest geopolitical catastrophe of the century, setting thus the course of Russian foreign policy towards great power status including neo-imperialist aspirations (Dettke 2011: 130). As some analysts have pointed out, after the 'colour revolutions', Russia has abandoned the idea of the CIS as a liberal trade community and there has been a consistent effort to reassert Russia's traditional sphere of influence (Dimitrova and Dragneva 2009: 864). The protracted conflicts in the former Soviet republics played an important role in this context.

For the Kremlin, the secessionist conflicts are an important instrument for keeping its grip on the 'near abroad'. Moscow uses them in order to prevent the advent of any hostile bloc or organisation towards its borders and put a great pressure on the former Soviet republics. The secessionist regions in the 'near abroad' are characterised by a general lack of democratic progress. The external (Russian) support is the only one that keeps them alive and thriving. The breakaway regions are aware of their dependence on Russian support, and consequently, allow Moscow a significant say on their internal matters. Hence, on the one hand, the Kremlin's support to the secessionist regions creates increasingly 'undemocratic reserved policy domains' within the former Soviet republics that severely restrict the effective power to rule of the democratically elected central governments of the former Soviet republics (Tolstrup 2009: 936). On the other hand, neither NATO nor the EU are willing to integrate states with internal territorial disputes. Therefore, by supporting the secessionist conflicts in the former Soviet republics, Moscow keeps a great leverage over both the internal and external policies of its neighbours.

Whenever Russia perceives its interests at stake in a former Soviet republic, the secessionist card becomes an efficient instrument for Moscow to try to 'convince' the small neighbour to take into account the Kremlin's concerns. Thus, on 25–27 January 2005, just days after the end of the 'orange revolution', the leaders of secessionist Transnistria, Abkhazia and South Ossetia met in Moscow with the Russian First Deputy Minister of Foreign Affairs, Valery Loshchinin and with Duma chairman, Boris Gryzlov. Two months later, leaders of Abkhazia, South Ossetia and Nagorno-Karabakh came again to Moscow, where they met separately with the Russian presidential administration, government, military and Duma officials. These meetings took place not at all at random; on the contrary, they were meant to warn the former Soviet republics in negotiations of protracted conflicts in Moldova and Caucasus.

Seeing its geopolitical interests endangered in Ukraine after the 'orange revolution', Russia sought to warm the separatist card in Crimea too. The Kremlin intensified its passportisation policy and three extremist pro-Russian youth movements opened branches in the Ukrainian peninsula: the Eurasian Youth Union – a subdivision of the international movement founded by Russian nationalist Alexander Dugin, a Moscow State University professor with close ties to the Kremlin (Shekhovtsov and Umland 2009); Proryv and Nashy, both with branches in Transnistria, Ankhazia and South Ossetia.

A more recent instrumentalization of the secessionist conflicts was noticed in the Republic of Moldova too. After the country overcame the 2013 political crisis, succeeding in establishing a new pro-European coalition government, in May 2013, the breakaway Transnistrian region promulgated a law on the 'State Border', transforming the administrative line into a political frontier. Two weeks later, after Moldova announced the completion of negotiations on the Deep and Comprehensive Free Trade Area, as part of the Association Agreement with the EU, the media announced that a group of Moldovan citizens from the autonomous region of Gagauzia had gathered signatures for a referendum on the independence of this territory. The two events came within the context of Moldova's intensified relations with the EU and the approach of the EaP Vilnius summit; and fit the pattern of Moscow's foreign policy of using the card of territorial integrity in the 'near abroad' for ensuring its strategic interests.

As the above examples show, Russia's coercive actions in the 'near abroad' fit the logic of realist zero-sum game. Moscow's assertive actions in its immediate neighbourhood have grown in intensity in the moments when the former Soviet republics were getting closer to the EU, NATO or the US. Even if the Kremlin's actions in the former Soviet space were alienating the local populations, Moscow was more interested in impeding those countries from getting closer to any other regional pole than Russia than to secure the sympathy of its neighbours.

3.   Estranging the 'near abroad', propelling the Eastern Partnership

The former Soviet space is perceived by the Kremlin as paramount for its security and economic stability. Therefore, especially since the beginning of the 2000s, Moscow has sought to prevent the former Soviet countries from moving closer to the West and to secure its energy transition to the European market. However, Russia's assertive policy towards the 'near abroad' did not achieve fully the expected results. If Russia tried to impose itself on its neighbours, especially by using economic tools, these were the same means that in fact estranged the former Soviet republics from Moscow, making them look to the West for guarantees of their sovereignty.

Russia's oil and gas exports have been the main factors of its economic revival and reassertion as a great power in the international arena. Therefore, ensuring the unimpeded transit of its gas and oil across the territories of the former Soviet republics to the European Union in particular, preventing the construction of pipelines to the EU outside its territory and gaining access to the CIS countries' own energy and other important resources represent paramount issues for Russia's might and stability, as losing its position on the European market and the monopoly on export routes would put Russia in the situation of competing with other export outlets (Aydın and Kaptanolu 2008: 766). On the other hand, by raising gas prices for the former Soviet republics, even for the most loyal ones, Russia sought to show its neighbours 'who is the boss' in the region, to pump more money into the federal budget and to force these countries to sell Russia their strategic assets, especially in the energy arena. However, Moscow's heavy-handedness undercut its influence with its neighbours, pushing them to seek closer relations with the West. The gas offensive did nothing but worry the former Soviet republics that Russia may use their energy dependency to interfere in their domestic affairs or to put pressure on them to make more and more foreign policy concessions (Woehrel 2009: 1). As a result, the aggressive Russian 'energodiplomacy' towards Ukraine, Moldova, Georgia, Armenia, Azerbaijan and Belarus gave an added momentum to these countries' interests in forging closer relations with NATO, the EU and the USA (Rumer 2007: 27), hoping that this could strengthen their sovereignty. Gazprom's demands for a gas price hike, for instance, have prompted unprecedented debates in Armenia about the value of the strategic partnership with Russia and shocked Belarus, setting the stage for these countries to join the EaP.

There was an even more dangerous perception of Moscow's asset-for-debt strategy. While Russia's policy of buying strategic assets in the CIS countries helps the Kremlin to play the modern integration game—political integration as a consequence of economic integration and not vice versa, a strategy that allows Russian capital to simply swallow economies of the former Soviet republics (Nygren 2008: 221)—this fact rouses concerns of the former Soviet republics that by controlling strategic assets in their countries, Russia would be able to manipulate the internal political situation, restraining thus their sovereignty. The situation was getting more tense given the fact that all these states have built their statehood in opposition to Russia (Trenin 2009: 19) and in the context of Putin's declaration about the collapse of the Soviet Union as the greatest geopolitical disaster of the century, read by many analysts as a '[setting] of the course of Russian foreign policy toward great power status including neo-imperialist aspirations'(Dettke 2011: 130), there were no doubts that the Kremlin would not hesitate to infringe their sovereignty whenever it considers its interests to be at stake.

As a result, even Putin's ties with Lukashenko became testy. The political union between Russia and Belarus did not move closer to realisation; ties with Moldova became damaged too, the communist president Voronin declaring officially his European aspirations; Azerbaijan continued to carefully establish closer relations with the West (it supplied cheap energy to Georgia, participated in GUAM, cooperated militarily with the United States), taking care, at the same time, not to exacerbate friction with Russia (Stent 2008: 1101); Ukraine and Georgia were pushing for NATO membership and expressed European aspirations, while Armenia was questioning the strategic partnership with Russia.

Russia's relationship with the 'near abroad' was stained even more by the 'economic wars'. While the increase of gas prices could have been 'accepted' as a 'need' to regulate the relations of independency between Russia and the CIS countries, the adjustment to the market price being proof of strictly economic cooperation, in the case of the 'food wars' or the expulsion of Georgians from Russia no one doubted the punitive nature of those actions. For the affected countries those were attempts of state destabilisation, while for the other former Soviet republics — warnings that Russia has no hesitation to use any means for securing its loyalty even if it meant destabilising or alteration of its neighbours' sovereignty. Thus, these economic wars have succeeded in estranging even Russia's union partner, Belarus, where the dictatorial and culturally Soviet president Lukashenko became father of national independence (Trenin 2009: 19). During the 'milk war', he accused Russia of trying to take control of Belarus' industries and destroy its sovereignty, adding that a confederation with Russia and Belarus would create 'another Chechnya', suggesting that Belarus would use military force to defend its independence (Gutterman 2009), and that 'Belarus is conducting its own independent domestic and foreign policy' and that it 'did not want to become an appendage of Russia, particularly an economic one', according to a member of Belarusian Parliament (Barry 2009). Thus, instead of keeping the former Soviet republics close, the 'economic wars' led to more estrangement and independence of these countries from Russia. Dependent on the Russian market for their exports, after the trade wars, the small neighbours concentrated their efforts on seeking other markets, and soon Russia lost its status of main trade partner in countries like Ukraine and Moldova, in favour of the EU.

Along with the economic problems generated by trade embargoes, energy dependence and discrediting of transit countries, the possession of strategic assets in the near abroad, the Russian 'game' in the protracted conflicts had also contributed to the alienation of the former Soviet republics from the West. The Kozak memorandum, Russian proposal of managing the Transnistrian issue, was the factor that determined the Moldovan Communist government to U-turn the country's foreign policy towards European integration. Showing clearly how little price Moscow was putting on Moldova's sovereignty through the Kremlin's plan of asymmetric federalisation of the former Soviet republic (Gomboş and Mateescu 2012: 56), Russia achieved nothing but encourage Chişinău to look towards the West for guarantees of its independence. Georgia, Armenia and Azerbaijan showed similar reactions, especially after the 2006 meetings of the separatist leaders in Moscow. Being clear that Russia was using the separatist conflicts against the central governments of the former Soviet republics, these countries sought rapprochement with NATO and the EU for solving their protracted conflicts.

The 2008 Georgian war affected Russia's relations with the CIS countries even more, alarming the former Soviet countries that have large ethnic minorities of potential secessionist problems, renewing the fear of Russian hegemony in the post-Soviet space (Light 2010: 237).

4.   A coincidence of needs and interests

The estrangement of the 'near abroad' and the former Soviet republics' choice of rapprochement with the West coincided with the EU's growing interest towards this region. The 2004–2007 enlargements brought new Eastern neighbours on the EU's borders, and made the EU a Black Sea power. However, not only did this extension grow the EU's influence and importance in the international arena; it brought also new threats and responsibilities, as 'what happens in the countries in Eastern Europe and the Southern Caucasus affects the European Union (...) their security, stability and prosperity increasingly impact on the EU's' (EEAS). Therefore, in order to ensure its own security Brussels had to ensure stable governance on its borders, and thus had to address the threats that came from the new Eastern neighbours, such as poverty, migration, transnational crime, etc. (Flenley 2008: 190). In 2004, the EU launched the European Neighbourhood Policy 'with the objective of avoiding the emergence of new dividing lines between the enlarged EU and [the new] neighbours and instead strengthened the prosperity, stability and security of all' (European Commission), seeking thus to extend a European 'postmodern' security community across the EU and create a 'ring of well governed countries' (Averre 2009: 1690).

The commitment to the European ideals, principles and community of values of the 'near abroad' highlighted by the 'colour revolutions' along with Russia's aggressive offensive that followed, presented the EU with the need for a more focused strategy on the Eastern neighbours. Russia's attempts to destabilise the economies of these countries and the danger of warming of the 'frozen conflicts' put at risk the stability and security of the EU. Furthermore, the 2008 Georgian War presented the former Soviet republics with a great dilemma: how to ensure their own security (Lukianov 2008a), and at the same time alerted the EU about how far the Kremlin is prepared to go in its policies towards the 'near abroad'. It was obvious that a greater involvement from Brussels in the Eastern neighbourhood was both expected and needed.

Furthermore, the gas crises had a major impact not only on the former Soviet republics but on the EU too. In January 2006, the European actors became aware of the fragility of European energy security. The Ukraine-Russian gas crisis came as a cold shower for the EU, which for the first time expressed its concern about predictions that by 2020 Russia would supply 70% of European gas imports. Within this context, in just a few months, Brussels' agenda dramatically changed; energy security became a top priority for the EU (Lussac 2010: 619), with Brussels making it clear that energy had to become a central component of all external relations (Sierra 2010:

650). The trend was enhanced even more by the January 2009 gas crisis, which reconfirmed the unreliability of the EU's Russian partner.

The crucial external goal of EU energy policy became the security of energy import supplies, understood as the reliable and predictable delivery of growing volumes of energy resources at acceptable prices (Kaveshnikov 2010: 592), in the Commission's (2006a: 3) words, '[when] EU citizens and businesses enjoy all the benefits of security of supply and lower prices'. For achieving this goal, the EU set some important measures that had to be implemented, summarised very well by Padgett (2011): 1) the reduction of the risk of import dependency by creating a fully integrated and competitive market that should allow member states to share and trade energy more flexibly, the interconnection of electric grids and pipelines mitigating also the impact of supply interruptions and overdependence on a single supplier (Ratner, Belkin, Nichol and Woerel 2012: 2); 2) the diversification of the EU's energy sources of supply by accessing Caspian and Central Asian resources. The importance of the Southern Corridor became crucial for the diversification of the EU's energy imports, this region being the only one where Europe can further diversify its gas imports, because of the peculiarities of gas transportation. As long as liquefied gas is more expensive and available only in limited amounts, the gas 'compressed' through pipelines remains the main source and the Caspian Basin offers large reserves from where the gas is still feasible to connect to Europe via pipelines (Sierra 2010: 650); 3) the creation of a wider European market that would enhance the security of supply, based on the assumption that 'well-functioning world markets are the best way of ensuring safe and affordable energy supplies' (Commission 2006b: 2). However, in order to create a wider European market, the EU needed to convince the non-member countries to adapt their energy sector to the internal European market and to '[create] a 'common regulatory space' around Europe [that] would imply progressively developing common trade, transit and environmental rules, market harmonisation and integration, [and that] would create a predictable and transparent mar-

ket to stimulate investment and growth, as well as security of supply, for the EU and its neighbours' (Commission 2006a: 16). In order
to reach this purpose, a set of institutions for cooperation with the
EU's neighbours were created to meet the needs of consumer, pro-
ducer and transit countries. This tactic is consistent with EU's philosophy of liberal institutionalism that suggests that institutions
shape countries' behaviour and the intensity of influence of institutions is directly proportional to their density.

Thus, the first important step in this respect was the establishment, in July 2006 of the EU-initiated Energy Community. The organisation is based on the EU energy *acquis* and was designed primarily for the neighbours in southeastern Europe (Padgett 2011:
1066). Its aim was to bind the non-member states to the EU without
offering them the possibility of admission to EU institutions. In
other words, for its own security, the EU was seeking to export the
acquis communitaire in the area of energy into the legislation of East
European countries, in the framework of the European Neighbourhood Policy.

The 2009 gas crisis gave an even stronger impetus to the EU's
policy of energy 'securitisation' through the export of its norms and
values to the Eastern neighbours. Already in a February 2009
speech, the Commissioner for Trade and European Neighbourhood
Policy, Benita Ferrero-Waldner, was emphasising that 'When Russia cuts gas supplies to Ukraine … EU households suffered. The EU
found its quality of life directly affected … by the political and commercial landscape in its eastern neighbourhood', going on to project
that in this context, 'it is important . . . we have partners whose governance provides respect for the rule of law' (Christou 2010: 418).
Within this context, the Eastern Partnership should be seen to be of
strategic importance in the energy sector too. Tying gas producers
(Azerbaijan) and transit countries (Georgia and Ukraine) more
closely to the EU, putting a great importance on energy security (see
EaP's platform 3), the EaP becomes an important instrument for expanding the EU's energy community and provides a greater energy
security and supplier diversification (Neuman 2010: 351). The replacing of old PCAs with Association Agreements offers the EU the

opportunity to convince the Eastern partners to adapt their legislation to the *acquis communautaire* leading to the creation of a free trade area between the EU and the partners, the implementation of mobility and security pacts and the safety of energy supply, the final objective being to establish a Neighbourhood Economic Community (Lussac 2010: 620).

However, if the EU member states succeed in their diversification efforts in securing energy sources, especially natural gas, this would reduce asymmetric ties with Russia as an energy supplier (Kirchner and Berk 2010: 860–861) and even possibly decrease the Kremlin's power in the international arena, based on Nye's (2005: 202) theory that 'manipulating the asymmetries of interdependence can be a source of power in international politics'. From Russia's perspective such a scenario is unacceptable. It would incline the balance of power in international affairs in favour of the EU and would significantly weaken its influence in the 'near abroad', which resides rather from pressure (economic, political, military) than from attractiveness and cooperation. Hence, the conflicting perceptions of Russia and the EU towards the EaP.

Conclusions

After the dissolution of the Soviet Union, Russia has sought to keep its influence in the 'near abroad' both for its own security and for the desired status of 'not just a big nation-state' but 'a pole in a multipolar world' (Popescu and Wilson 2009: 7). Domestic problems and a lack of resources undermined this aim in the 1990s, however. It was only after 2000 that Moscow had the necessary means for pursuing the policy of regaining its lost positions in the CIS. Yet, the gas wars, the acquisition of the strategic assets of the former Soviet republics, trade boycotts, political discourse about the fall of the Soviet Union as a great geopolitical catastrophe put on alert both the countries of the 'near abroad' and the EU.

While Russia's assertive policy in the 'near abroad', translated in asymmetric federalisation plans (the Kozak memorandum), energy blackmail or attempts at economic disruptions, sought to strengthen the dependence of the 'near abroad' on Russia and to discredit the former Soviet republics, creating thus the circumstances that would have allowed the Kremlin to easily influence the internal and external policies of its neighbours; Moscow's actions have instead raised suspicions in the former Soviet republics about Russia's viability as strategic partner. Furthermore, instead of moving closer to its neighbours, 'energodiplomacy' and the economic wars have made the former Soviet republics look for rapprochement with the EU and NATO, as guarantors of their sovereignty. Within this context, we can conclude that the EaP emerged not only from the EU's need to build 'a ring of friends' around its Eastern borders, but also in response to the demands of the countries from the 'common neighbourhood' for greater EU involvement in this area.

Chapter 6
Russia's Relations with the EaP Countries after 2009

Introduction

The EaP did not only change Moscow's attitude towards the EU, whom it started to perceive as a major rival in the 'near abroad' but in the logic of zero-sum game, it increased also Russia's preoccupation for the six former Soviet republics, members of this European initiative: Belarus, Moldova, Ukraine, Georgia, Armenia and Azerbaijan. Generally, one can notice that the increase in Russian presence in the area is directly linked with the progress of the former Soviet republics in the framework of the EaP. As the empirical data show, even if at the beginning of the EaP, Moscow did not express too much concern regarding the rapprochement of these countries towards the EU, once they were showing more willingness to conclude Association Agreements with the EU, the Kremlin's foreign policy in the 'near abroad' became more assertive.

1. Russia and the EaP countries

1.1 Belarus

Constructing their identity and sovereignty in opposition to Russia but dependent on Russian market and subsidies, Minsk has seen the EaP as a perfect opportunity for counterbalancing Russian vector in its foreign policy. It is hard to believe that President Lukashenko took into serious the implementation of the reforms implied by its membership in the EU-led initiative, given that the democratization of the country would have jeopardized his personal political stance. Most probably Lukashenko sought to take advantage of the EaP membership to strengthen Minsk's positions in the relationship with Russia.

The political decision of becoming member of the EU initiative—an act of defying the Eastern regional hegemon—led to a worsening of the relations between Minsk and Moscow. The two countries had already been at odds after the 2008 Georgian war, when Belarus, a member of union state with Russia, refused to recognize the independence of Abkhazia and South Ossetia. In practical terms, the worsening of Belarus-Russia relations was felt in Minsk through economic pressure and media campaign against the incumbent political leadership. In June 2009, Moscow imposed a ban on Belarusian milk and other some 500 dairy products, invoking their failure to meet Russian hygiene and production standards. The announcement was made just a day after President Lukashenko accused Russia of using economic aid to put pressure on Belarus to recognize Abkhazia and South Ossetia. The sanctions had a great impact on Belarus' economy given the fact that only in 2008 the former Soviet republic earned $1 billion from its exports of milk to Russia (Johnson 2009).

Minsk remained part of the Customs Union with Russia and Kazakhstan, however, the tense atmosphere with Moscow continued. In 2010, during the presidential election campaign in Belarus, the Russian major television channel NTV, that broadcasts in Belarus too, featured a documentary 'The God Father.' The movie portrayed Lukashenko as an unscrupulous dictator determined to stay in power at any costs and presented the numerous human rights violations committed during his presidency.

To the satisfaction of Russia, Belarus' pro-EU vector did not last too long. The end of 2010 already announced a shift in Minsk's foreign policy. After the December crackdown of the post-electoral protests and the subsequent harsh criticism of EU political leaders, Lukashenko sought a rapprochement with Russia. This turning point was not motivated only by Brussels' criticism on democracy situation in Belarus but rather by economic aspects. During the 2010 presidential campaign Lukashenko ordered a 50 per cent increase in wages of all workers in the state sector. This populist decision led the country to a crisis by March 2011, with the currency in collapse and shortages through the economy. Belarus was in a desperate need of financial help, and as the relations with the West were damaged after the crackdown of the 2010 protests, Minsk had no other choice but to turn towards Russia for support. And, after several months of wait, in November 2011, Moscow announced a rescue plan for Belarus of $3 billion from the Eurasian Economic Community Bail-out Fund and $1 billion from Russian state owned Sberbank. In exchange, Minsk agreed to sell the remaining shares in Beltransgas (Belarus pipeline company) to Gazprom (Shoemaker 2014: 159) and Minsk had not shown any sign of progress within the EaP.

That Belarus re-entered in Russia's good graces was demonstrated also by the fact that the first foreign visit of Vladimir Putin after he began the third presidential mandate was in Minsk. Moreover, during that official trip Russian President and Aleksandr Lukashenko released a joint statement that criticised the EU sanctions on Belarus and underlined that the two countries 'will coordinate efforts to counter attempts to interfere in the internal affairs of the Union State and apply pressure through the introduction of restrictive measures or sanctions' (Reuters 2012).

Yet, Belarus-Russia relations have not been smooth for too long. The pressure of Russian company Uralkali on Minsk to sell Belaruskali, Belarus Potash Company, determined Lukashenko to arrest in 2013 the general director of the Uralkali, after a meeting of the latter with the Belarusian prime minister. In response, the Russian government banned the import of Belarusian hogs and pork products and announced a 20 percent reduction in oil exports to Belarus (Shoemaker 2014: 159). This crisis was overcome only after President Putin ordered an investigation into the general director of the Uralkali on suspicion of abuse in power.

Balancing between Russia and the EU, Belarus has not expressed too much willingness towards the cooperation within the EEU either. In 2014, Minsk was on the brink of not signing the Eurasian Union Treaty because of the misunderstandings on oil duties. On the other side, Russia disregarded Belarus' interests as a member of the EEU as well. Moscow has taken several unilateral economic decisions that affected the other member states of the union: imposed economic sanctions on Moldova, Ukraine and Georgia and boycotted the food imports from the EU countries. Then, after Russian authorities found out some attempts of re-exporting of EU fruits and vegetable via Belarus, in December 2014, Russia re-stricted the transit of Belarusian cargo, banned several Belarusian producers, and there were reinstalled border controls.

Belarus' relations with Russia were even more poisoned after the annexation of Crimea. In the expansionist fervour some Russian commentators suggested that once the Ukrainian peninsula 'came back,' Belarus should join Russia or might face territorial disinte-gration in case of a clash between the West and Russia. For Moscow, reunification of Russian historical territories 'is not a whim or im-perial feature is a historical need', Russia being the 'only guarantor of the Russian world and therefore of Belarus and Malorussia [Ukraine]' (Birov 2015). Others insisted that Russia should reex-amine the legality of 'ceding of Western provinces of RSFSR to Bel-arus' (Averyano-Minskii 2015). These views infuriated Luka-shenko, who declared that in case of aggravation of the situation he was ready to arm half million of Belarusians (Independent 2015). Minsk also banned from entering the country some of the Kremlin's advisors who made remarks on Belarus' independence and territo-rial integrity.

At the moment of writing this book, Belarus-Russia relations remain quite tense. Even if the two countries are members of the same customs union, the border controls reinstalled in December 2014 are still in force. Minsk has tried recently to balance its foreign policy towards the EU. After Belarus did not recognize the annexa-tion of Crimea and refused to apply sanctions on EU food exports, Minsk tried to position itself as a mediator between Russia and the West throughout the Ukraine crisis and hosted the talks on the cease-fire agreement in Donbas.

1.2 The Republic of Moldova

Since its independence, the Republic of Moldova has oscillated be-tween the rapprochement with Russia and the West. The year 2009 found the country in a pro-Moscow phase of its foreign policy. The so-called 'Twitter revolution' against rigged elections, in April 2009, determined the Communist government in Chișinău to look for closer relations with the Russian Federation for support and legitimisation. President Voronin interpreted the social unrest in Moldova as a coup d'état organized by the neighbouring Romania, expelled the Romanian Ambassador, introduced visas for Romanian citizens, and transformed the country into an isolated fortress opened only to Russia. Moldova was, thus on the brink of becoming a 'new Belarus' at the EU's border (Rotaru 2014: 145). In its turn, the Kremlin expressed its official support for Moldovan Communists and despite numerous violations of human rights during the 'Twitter Revolution,' Russian President Medvedev congratulated his Moldovan counterpart on how he acted during the violent protests on April 7, 'which permitted maintaining control of the state of things and to restoring law and order in the capital city' (e-democracy 2009).

However, this close rapprochement with Russia did not last too long. As the Party of Communists missed one vote for electing the president of Moldova and failed twice to do so, the government had to organize new elections, in July 2009. This time, the opposition parties succeeded in forming a coalition government, entitled the Alliance for European Integration, and sent the pro-Russian communists into opposition. Yet, the new government was not able to elect the president either and had to organize new early parliamentary elections in November 2010. The Alliance for European Integration was re-created and in March 2012, it was able to elect the former head of Supreme Court of Magistrates, Nicolae Timofti, in the Presidential chair of the country. As the name of the governmental coalition suggests, Moldova reconfigured its foreign policy on a pro-Western vector.

The two general elections of July 2009 and November 2010 have an important element in common: both times, like in a reproduced scenario, the following week after the poll, the Kremlin sent the head of the Administration of the President of Russian Federation, Sergey Naryshkin, to manage a pro-Russian government coalition. Both in 2009 and 2010, Naryshkin tried to convince the Democratic Party of Moldova to ally with the Party of Communists, promising in exchange the reduction in gas price, the resumption of imports of Moldovan wine and support in the Transnistrian settlement process. Without result though.

In 2013 in the prospect of the Vilnius EaP Summit, Russia became more assertive towards the Republic of Moldova. Moscow warned the authorities in Chișinău that an AA with the EU would bring economic 'consequences' from Russian part. As Moldovan government continued negotiations with the EU, the Kremlin started first to re-activate the secessionist card, then to use the economic tools. In June 2013, the breakaway Transnistria adopted a law on 'state border' that included tree villages that were not previously under the control of the secessionist region. Two weeks later, in the Autonomous Territorial Unit of Gagauzia there were gathered signatures for a referendum on independence.

In September 2013, Rospotrebnadzor, Russian Federal Service for Surveillance on Consumer Rights Protection and Human Well-being, 'discovered' that Moldovan wines contained traces of harmful chemical substances and imposed a total ban of imports of Moldovan wine and spirits. (It is to mention that the previous ban on Moldovan wine, imposed in 2006, has never been totally lifted, however, gradually some companies had obtained the right to export wine products to Russia). This measure cost Moldova only in a couple of moths $6.6 million (The Economist 2013).

At the beginning of June 2014, on the eve of signing the AA with the EU the Moldovan media disclosed the details of a secret meeting between the Governor of Gagauzia, a Moldovan Metropolitan Bishop (subordinated to the Russian Patriarchate) and the leader of the Party of Patriots of Moldova, that devised a plan to destabilize the situation in Moldova. According to the source, the three actors discussed the prospects of establishing of a separatist enclave in the South of Moldova – the 'People's Republic of Gagauzia' (that besides Moldovan southern raions should have comprised the Ukrainian regions of Bolgrad and Ismail); and a separatist region in the North – the 'North Moldavian Republic' (consisting of Moldovan Northern raions and Ukrainian region of Chernovtsy) (deschide.md 2014). In the same month, Moldovan authorities announced that had uncovered a scheme that involved officials from Gagauzia who recruited and facilitated youngsters from the region to pursue specializing training in military camps in Russia. Around 100 people would have received training in managing fire arms, building barricades and check points, techniques of sizing buildings and street fighting (Secrieru 2014: 1). In case of these new secessionist scenarios the control of the government of Chişinău would have been reduced to less than a third of the country, given that Moldova has another breakaway region in the Eastern part, Transnistria. Considering the involved actors and the context of the Ukrainian crisis it is not hard to figure out who was behind the threatening scenarios of territorial disintegration.

After on 27 June 2014, Moldova signed the AA with the EU, on 21 July, Russia imposed a ban on the imports of fruits from the former Soviet republic, and two days later expanded the prohibition on the canned fruits and vegetables and the processed meat. The ban was spread in October on all Moldovan meat products.

The November 2014 parliamentary elections in Moldova, occasioned new tensions between Moscow and Chişinău. Russia overtly disregarded the sovereignty of the smaller former Soviet republic and involved in the election campaign by financing the pro-Moscow party of Renato Usatyi, 'Fatherland.' As the legislation of Moldova does not allow a political formation to be financed by a foreign state, the central Election Commission banned 'Fatherland' days before the elections (in 2015, Usatyi succeeded in being elected the mayor of Moldova's second biggest city, Bălţi). Russia has also openly supported the election of Irina Vlah as the Governor of Gagauzia, successfully in this case.

Moldova-Russia relations have been also poisoned by Chişinău's ban of several Russian citizens to enter the former Soviet republic. Since the fall of 2014 a number of military men and journalists from Russia have been sent back from Moldovan airport and the director of the Russian international information agency "Russia Today," Dmitri Kiselyov and journalist Andrey Kondrashov were declared undesirable.

Yet, despite the political tensed relations between the two countries, Moldova served this period as a perfect place for criminal organisations and corrupt politicians from Russia to launder money. Between 2010–2014, almost $20 billion, illegal money coming from Russia, passed through Moldindconbank and were then spread through the whole Europe. Indeed, this could have not been done without the involvement of the local governing politicians. Consequently, the disclosure of the illegal financial activity resulted in discrediting of Moldovan banking system and of the 'pro-European' governing coalition. However, the investigation on money laundering was soon overshadowed by even worse financial scandal—the vanishing of $1 billion from three Moldovan banks. For tiny Moldova this loss represents about 15 per cent of its GDP and had a great potential of destabilizing the country. The investigation of this case is not over yet, however, some preliminary reports indicate that beyond the involvement of the Moldovan politicians from power, the clues lead also to Moldovan-Russian dual citizenship individuals living in Russia (BBC 2015). We do not have enough data to assess whether Russia has any involvement in this case, yet we could not ignore that the vanishing of the $1 billion offers Moscow good opportunities to strengthen its positions in the former Soviet republic.

The protests held in Moldova over the disappearance of the billion US dollars have not been ignored by Moscow. Russian state-controlled TV outlets have broadcasted reports that depicted the social unrest as being caused by the rapprochement of Moldova with the EU, which would have brought economic dissatisfaction because of the tough conditions of the AA and West's support for the corrupt 'pro-EU' governance. The pro-Moscow Renato Usatyi (Our Party) and Igor Dodon (Party of Socialists) attempted to confiscate the protests and to direct them from the anti-corruption message towards the Eurasian integration vector, however, they have been unsuccessful.

In November 2016, the pro-Russian leader of the Party of Socialists, Igor Dodon, was elected as the president of the Republic of Moldova. Yet, with limited powers (Moldova is a parliamentary republic) he has not been able to significantly change the foreign policy of his country. The biggest achievement in Dodon's relations with the Russian Federation has been obtaining the status of observer country of Moldova in the EEU. However, this is a rather symbolic gesture, the government of Chişinău keeps expressing a pro-EU rhetoric.

1.3 Georgia

The war of August 2008 resulted in the freeze of Georgia-Russia relations. The tension between the two countries reached the highest level since their independence. On 26 August 2008, the Kremlin recognized unilaterally the independence of breakaway Abkhazia and South Ossetia. In response, Georgia suspended the diplomatic relations with Russia. The political leaders in Moscow and Tbilisi switched then to personal attacks and undiplomatic insults. Russian Prime-Minister Vladimir Putin said that he wanted to hang up Georgian President by the genitals, Saaakashvilli mocked at Putin's short stature, calling him Lilli-Putin.

The war and the subsequent recognition of Abkhazia and South Ossetia blocked Georgia's plans to apply for NATO membership. However, at the same time, these actions resulted in a major loss of Russian influence in the Caucasus country. Within a climate of hatred, the Georgian authorities started even actively replacing the Russian with English as first the foreign language in schools and in the public sphere. In addition, Tbilisi was using its veto right to prevent Russia from finalizing its long-lasting negotiations with the WTO.

At the end of 2011, the relations between Tbilisi and Moscow appeared to improve. In December, within the context of US-Russia reset, the West convinced Georgia to lift its veto on Russian membership in the WTO. Two month later, in February 2012, President Saakashvilli even suggested in a discourse in front of the Georgian parliament that his country could grant visa-free travel regime for Russian citizens. This change in Tbilisi's stance was answered through a statement on the website of Russian Ministry of Foreign Affairs announcing that Russia was 'ready to introduce a mutual visa-free regime for the Georgian citizens' and proposed 'to re-establish diplomatic relations between [the two] countries' (mid.ru 2012). However, the next day, President Saakashvilli rejected the terms of Russia's offer, insisting that in order to restore the diplomatic relations, Russia had first to recognize Abkhazia and South Ossetia as part of Georgia (Shoemaker 2014: 244).

The election campaign in Georgia offered Moscow a good opportunity to regain ground in the Caucasus republic. In October 2011, and then in September 2012, just before the parliamentary elections 'Ukrainian Wikileaks,' an obscure website registered in Russia, leaked videos showing inmates being tortured and raped by guards in Georgian prisons (civil.ge 2012). These footages discredited Saakashvilli government and prompted spontaneous protests in Tbilisi. The events had a decisive contribution to the victory of Georgian Dream opposition bloc of Bidzina Ivanishvilli.

The change in power in 2012, appeared promising for Georgia-Russia relations. The victory of the bloc coalition of Bidzina Ivanishvilli, a Georgian billionaire who made his money in Russia and relied in the election campaign on the message of the improvement of relations with Russia, announced a more flexible foreign policy. It is true that, to Moscow's disappointment, the Georgian new government reiterated Saakashvilli's core objectives—EU and NATO membership and the non-recognition of Abkhazia and South Ossetia, however, comparing to the previous Georgian political leadership there was not a negative background of the relationship with the Kremlin's leaders and the political message was directed clearly towards the normalisation of the relations with Russia.

Thus, in a step towards rebuilding the good relations, Tbilisi offered assistance to Moscow in providing security for the Winter Olympics in Sochi, and Georgian athletes participated at the event. In spring 2013, Russia lifted the ban on imports of Georgian mineral water and wine and partially on agricultural products. However, this trade improvement trend was short lived. In just few months, in October 2013, displeased that Tbilisi continued to seek rapprochement with the EU, Russian Rospotrebnadzor re-imposed the ban on the import of wines from seven Georgian producers. Moreover, after Georgia signed the AA with the EU, on 27 June 2014, Moscow warned that this would have 'serious consequences' (DW 2014).

Russia's relations with the secessionist Abkhazia and South Ossetia have also contributed to the poisoning of Tbilisi-Moscow affairs. The visit of President Putin in Abkhazia, in August 2013, where he met with his Abkhaz 'counterpart' to discuss the bilateral relations between Moscow and Sukhumi, fueled protests from Georgian government. Tbilisi condemned the visit as 'another infringement on Georgia's territorial integrity and sovereignty' (Sputniknews 2013). The annexation of Crimea, in March 2014, raised more suspicions in Tbilisi about Moscow's involvement with the two breakaway regions, which will be further increased by the strategic partnerships of Russia with Abkhazia and South Ossetia.

In November 2014, President Putin and the Abkhaz separatist leader Raul Khadzhimba signed the Agreement on Alliance and Strategic Partnership (after Sukhumi negotiated to change the title of the treaty from 'Integration' to 'Strategic Partnership'). The treaty envisages the creation of a common space of defence and security and a gradual merger of Abkhazian law enforcement, border, customs, economic and healthcare systems with those of Russia (Rukhadze 2015). Sukhumi also agreed to harmonise its foreign and defence policies with those of Russia, and Moscow promised economic support for the breakaway region.

At the first anniversary of the annexation of Crimea, on 18 March 2015, Russia signed a similar document with the second Georgian secessionist region, South Ossetia – the Agreement on Alliance and Integration. The treaty with Tskhinvali is even more assimilative. Besides the creation of a common defence and security space, it removed the restrictions on movement of people and goods, envisaged the integration of the customs bodies, expanded cooperation between the interior ministries of the two parts, and simplified the procedures for the acquiring of Russian citizenship. Georgian government protested against these treaties, accusing Russia of violation of Georgia's sovereignty and raised concerns about the possible annexation of these regions (Financial Times 2015).

Few months later, in July 2015, Russia-backed South Ossetia placed new 'border' markings, occupying territory beyond the disputed administrative boundary line. This way, a 1.5 km section of the Baku-Supsa pipeline of strategic importance for Tbilisi, passed under the control of the secessionist region (The Guardian 2015). These developments complicated both Georgia-Russia relations and the positions of the Dream Coalition government that committed to reduce tensions with Russia when took office in 2012.

Russia most probably does not have any intentions to annex the Georgian territories, however, the threat of possible grabbing of land has been a successful tool for putting pressure on Tbilisi. For instance, in October 2015, after Vladislav Surkov, a personal adviser of President Putin, visited South Ossetia, the breakaway region announced that it was planning a referendum of joining the Russian Federation. Moscow has not answered to those claims. Surkov's visit delivered most probably the permission for the separatist regime in Tskhinvali to raise the question of annexation as a tool to influence Tbilisi (Cecire 2015).

At the moment of writing this book, the diplomatic ties between Georgia and Russia are still suspended. However, at the end of 2015, Moscow showed a softening tone in its stance towards Tbilisi. In the December annual press conference, President Putin announced that Moscow was ready to cancel the visa regime with Georgia (Putin 2015a).

1.4 Armenia

Armenia is one of the most faithful Russian allies in the 'near abroad.' It is true that the geopolitical equation does not offer Yerevan too much choice in choosing 'friends'. Blocked by the protracted conflict over Nagorno-Karabakh, Armenia has sought the rapprochement with Moscow in the first place for security reasons. The former Soviet republic hosts one of the largest Russian military bases abroad, which guarantees the Kremlin that Yerevan stands no chance to join NATO or any other military organization Russia is not part of; and Armenia's borders with Turkey and Iran are guarded by Russian soldiers. In August 2010, Yerevan and Moscow signed a deal that extended the lease of Russian military base in Gyumri from 2020 to 2044 and committed Russia to provide Yerevan with modern weapons and equipment to its military.

However, this rapprochement has not exempted Armenia from Russian pressure. In May 2013, *Kavkaz Online* reported that in the political circles of Russia it was analysed the possibility of inclusion of Armenia into the Russian Federation and that existed already a prior consent on this from the President of Armenia Serzh Sargsyan (Kavkaz Online 2013). It is hard to believe that the Kremlin would have taken seriously into consideration such scenario, yet, only the spread of such thesis put pressure not only on Yerevan but on the other former Soviet republics as well. These threats on the sovereignty and even the independence of the Caucasus republic came within the context of Yerevan's plans to initiate an AA with the EU.

At the beginning Russia did not criticise Yerevan particularly for joining the EaP and did not object to its rapprochement with Brussels, however, when Armenia was getting closer to a new strategic agreement with the EU, the Kremlin changed its attitude. Throughout the spring and summer of 2013 both Yerevan and Brussels were showing expectations that the two parts would initiate the AA at the EaP Vilnius Summit. However, just two months before the November summit, Armenia announced a shift in its foreign policy. On 3 September 2013, Armenian president, Serj Sargsyan, made a working visit in Russia, where he met Vladimir Putin. After the meeting, Sargsyan surprised both domestic and EU audience by announcing the decision of Yerevan to join the Customs Union of Russia, Belarus and Kazakhstan. Armenian leader explained that 'since we share a system of military security, it is impossible and inefficient to isolate ourselves from the corresponding geo-economical space. This is a rational decision; it is a decision based on Armenia's national interests' (kremlin.ru 2013a). In order to understand better the decision of Yerevan we should look at a broader context of the spring-summer of 2013. Short after *Kavkaz Online* reported about the possibility of incorporation of Armenia into the Russian Federation, Moscow announced its intentions to increase the price of its gas exports to Armenia. Then, in June 2013, Russia delivered a large amount of arms to Azerbaijan, worth $1 billion, based on an agreement signed a year ago. Two months after, during a meeting with Russian President Putin in Baku, the Azeri President disclosed the price of the arms deal with Moscow: 'the military and technical cooperation with Russia is measured at $4 billion and it tends to grow further' (Blomberg 2013). The news put a great pressure on Yerevan, especially considering that the neighbouring Azerbaijan boosted its military spending and has reiterated its intentions of not to exclude military actions for settling the Nagorno-Karabakh dispute. Within this context, Armenia's decision to join the Customs Union proved once again the effectiveness of both the economic and secessionist cards for Russian foreign policy in the 'near abroad.'

Yerevan's decision to join the Customs Union was 'rewarded' by Moscow. In December 2013, Armenia signed a five-year agreement with Gazprom that secured the base price of Russian gas at $189/tmc. In exchange, Russian state-company purchased the last 20% Yerevan's shares of joint Russian-Armenian natural gas pipelines company, ArmRosgazprom, and renamed the company Gazprom Armenia.

On 2 January 2015, Armenia became the forth member-state of the EEU. However, soon Yerevan's relations with Russia were shaken by the murder of an Armenian family of seven members including a two-year-old girl and a six-month-old boy by a Russian soldier from the military base in Gyumri. Moscow's refusal to let the suspect tried in an Armenian court provoked massive protests by Armenians and clashes with the police. In the summer of 2015, Yerevan was the scene of unprecedented protests generated by the decision of Armenian Electricity Network, a subsidiary of the Russian company Inter RAO UES, to raise the electricity tariff with 6 drams. These social protests undermined the public trust in the strategic alliance with Russia. Probably for regaining sympathy of the Armenian society, during the summer protests, Moscow agreed to have the suspect of the massacre in Gyumri tried by an Armenian court.

Blocked by the protracted conflict of Nagorno-Karabkh, Armenia has no other choice but to maintain close relations with Russia. However, as the above examples show, Yerevan is not hesitating to balance Moscow's influence whenever the international context allows.

1.5 Azerbaijan

Azerbaijan's relations with Russia are determined to a large extent by the Nagorno-Karabakh issue as well. Moscow's support for Armenia's security and military capabilities are carefully followed by the Baku government. At the beginning of 2009, for instance, Azerbaijan showed its discontent with the allegations that Russia had transferred weapons worth $800 million to Armenia the previous year. Officially, the Kremlin denied the facts, however, Russian defence minister, Serdyukov allegedly admitted later the transfer (The Guardian 2009).

Taking advantage of Baku's concerns about its military security, the fragile equilibrium of the Caucasus and Azerbaijani's revenues from exports of oil and gas, Russia uses also Azerbaijan as a lucrative market for its military equipment. In 2011–2012 the two countries signed several contracts for Russian tanks, rocket launchers and artillery cannons. Azeri president disclosed the value of the arms deals with Moscow to $4 billion (see above).

Beyond the military issues, Russia has a particular interest in Azerbaijan's hydrocarbon resources. In 2009 Moscow signed with Baku an agreement on importing Azeri gas and in 2010 Russia imported almost one billion cubic meters and increased the volumes the following years. According to specialists, for Gazprom, which re-exports the gas bought from Azerbaijan to Europe, this is not a lucrative business. It is cheaper to produce gas domestically, however, for Russia the principle that the more gas it buys from Azerbaijan, the less the others (the EU) can buy appears to be more important (Shoemaker 2014: 227), as it prevents Europe from diversifying its energy sources.

Overall, Azerbaijan has not been too willing to develop a very close relationship with Russia, both because of Moscow's support for Armenia and because of Baku's cooperation with Turkey, however, the Kremlin is not worried about Azerbaidjan's foreign policy. Even if the country is a member of the EaP, it has not responded positively to EU standards spill-over processes, Azerbaijan has constantly showed disappointment on EU's approach towards the region of Nagorno-Karabakh (Salvati 2015), and as long as the status quo of the protracted conflict is maintained, Azerbaijan cannot join NATO and Russia has a strong leverage on both Yerevan and Baku. In addition, Russia has sent Baku signals that it can encourage other secessionist troubles in the Caucasus republic if it is 'needed': in the southern part of Azerbaijan, where lives the Talysh minority; or in the north of the country, where Moscow supports the Avar and Lezgin minorities (Goble 2014).

As the empirical evidence indicates, in the relations with the former Soviet republics, Russia shows little concern about their sovereignty. Whether we analyse the cases of Moldova, Belarus or the Caucasus former Soviet republics, we find numerous examples of Russia's interference in domestic politics of these countries, the use of secessionist card or the economic pressure for influencing their foreign policies. However, if in the five countries analysed above Russia's infringement on sovereignty has been more covered, in Ukraine, Moscow has not refrained from open actions.

1.6. Ukraine

Russia's relationship with Ukraine experienced a tense period after the 'Orange Revolution'. Kiev was determined in pursuing a rapprochement with the EU and to Moscow's vocal dissatisfaction openly declared its intentions to join NATO. Within this context, in January 2009, Ukraine was hit by the most severe gas crisis. In full cold winter Russia's Gazprom cut off the supplies to Ukraine, because of the accumulating debts of the neighbouring country. This decision affected not only Ukraine but left without gas supplies the Southeastern Europe and other European countries that depended of Russian gas transported through the Ukrainian pipeline system. Only after 20 days the gas flows were restarted, after Russian prime-minister Vladimir Putin and his Ukrainian counterpart, Yulia Timoshenko, negotiated a new ten-years contract.

In May 2009 Ukraine joined the EaP and soon became the front-runner of the EU's initiative. Despite the political instability, Kiev was making great success in aligning with the European norms and standards and became the first EaP member state that initiated the AA with the EU, in March 2012.

The Ukrainian presidential election of 2010 brought to power the 'big loser' of the 'Orange Revolution', Viktor Yanukovych. This political change created a favorable climate for Russia-Ukraine relations. From the beginning Yanukovych announced that Kiev will continue its rapprochement with the EU but will remain a neutral country without any intentions to join neither NATO nor the CSTO. Yanukovych declared his readiness to consider the initiative of Russian president Medvedev on the European collective security system and showed his interest for the development of the economic relations with Russia (Kyiv Post 2010).

The first major sign of improvement of Ukrainian-Russian relations was the 'Gas for fleet' agreement. On 21 April 2010 the presidents of the two countries met in Kharkov and signed an extension to the lease on the Russian base in Sevastopol for 25 years, until 2042. In exchange, Kiev received a discount of $100 per thousand cubic meters of Russian gas. The deal saved Ukrainian budget billions, however, did not help Kiev to resolve the severe problems in its energy sector (Sakwa 2015: 71).

Even if at the declarative level, Yanukovych insisted on Ukraine's rapprochement with the EU, the empirical evidence showed little in this respect. Instead of complying with the assumed reforms, the democracy in Ukraine continued to deteriorate, the parliamentary elections in 2012 were largely manipulated. Already at the end of 2010 Europe was perceiving Yanukovych's regime as corrupt and authoritarian (Aslund 2015: 43). At the same time, however, Yanukovych firmly opposed the accession to Russia-led Customs Union. As Ukraine continued the negotiations with the EU on the signing of the AA at the Vilnius EaP summit, Russia started a trade war with the neighbouring Slavic country. In July 2013 Moscow imposed economic sanctions, banning the imports of a series of Ukrainian agricultural products, steel pipes, and chocolates. The following month, Russia blocked most of Ukrainian exports by putting Ukrainian companies that exported to Russia on a 'list of risk.' In September, Moscow blocked the imports of railway wagons. Meanwhile, a series of sharp warnings about major economic consequences that could accompany the potential signing of the AA with the EU were coming from Russia. Putin's adviser, Sergey

Glazyev drew attention that 'signing this treaty will lead to political and social unrest. The living standards will decline dramatically … there will be chaos' and because by signing the AA with the EU, Ukraine will 'violate the treaty of strategic partnership and friendship with Russia,' when the social unrest happened, 'Russia could no longer guarantee Ukraine's status as a state and could possibly intervene if pro-Russian regions of the country appealed directly to Moscow' (The Guardian 2013).

This pressure appeared not to prevent Kiev from signing the AA with the EU, tough. Weeks before the November EaP summit, president Yanukovych insisted that Ukraine needed the free trade agreement with the EU and 'by choosing to get closer to the European Union, we are making a pragmatic choice for optimal and rational modernization' (Bloomberg 2013). However, Ukraine was facing the third recession since 2008 and Yanukovych was worried in the perspective of the presidential elections of 2015. He needed urgent economic help, but soon realized that the EU was placing little on the table that would benefit immediately, while the reforms Ukraine would have to implement after signing the AA would most probably destabilise an already precarious situation (Sakwa 2015: 79). Moscow took advantage of Kiev's weakness and raised the offer.

On 9 November 2013, Viktor Yanukovych and Vladimir Putin met secretly on the territory of a military base in the suburbs of Moscow, where most probably Russian president presented some proposals the Ukrainian counterpart could not refuse. The following week the prime ministers of the two countries met in Saint Petersburg. As it was revealed later, Russia offered Kiev $15 billion immediate support and preferential gas tariffs. At his return from Russia, Ukraine's prime-minister Mykola Azarov, announced on 21 November 2013, that the Ukrainian government decided to 'suspend the process of preparation for the signing of the Association Agreement between Ukraine and the EU,' in order to take measure for 'insurance of the national security', to make 'a more detailed study of measures that have to be taken to compensate the loss from redirection of trade and economic relations' (Ukrainskaya Pravda 2013).

The announcement surprised the public opinion and came within the context of a worsening socio-economic situation in Ukraine, mass distrust of the state and political representative institutions, dissatisfaction of many interest groups isolated from decision-making, discontent of people regarding routine injustice and corruption, and the polarization of society towards the stance of Russian language in the cultural and administrative spheres (Stepanenko 2015: 37). This was the spark that brought people into the street.

On 21 November around 1,500 persons went to the Square of Independence in Kiev to protest against the government's decision to suspend the negotiations with the EU and about 150 of them remained there until the morning. It was a spontaneous manifestation, initiated by civic activists and students. On Saturday, 23 November, thousands of people gathered in the center of Kiev to express their support for the European integration. The majority of them were not so much angered by the halt of the negotiations with Brussels but by the cynical way it was communicated. The people were announced about the decision after the previous day the government had confirmed that they would most certainly be signing the agreement at the EU summit in Vilnius (Portnov and Portnova 2015: 59).

President Yanukovych went at the EaP Vilnius Summit, on 28-29 November 2013, however, he did not even sign the declaration of intent. During an unofficial discussion with the German Chancellor Angela Merkel he only complained that 'for three and a half years in very unequal conditions, [he alone withstood] a very strong Russia' (news.bigmir.net 2013).

In the night of 29-30 November 2013 Ukrainian government tried to disperse the manifestation in Kiev. Under the pretext of preparations for the erection of the New Year's tree the special police unit Berkut entered the Independence Square (Maidan Nezalezhnosti) generating violent confrontations. About 35 protesters were injured and 31 were detained by the police. It was for the first time when Ukrainian authorities used serious violence against the population. The event prompted the mobilization of more people and on 1 December over half million gathered in the center of Kiev where occupied the city hall and the Trade Union building and attempted to topple the statue of Lenin off the main street. The opposition called for national strike and started setting up tents in the Independence Square.

While protests continued, on 6 December President Yanukovych met in Sochi with Vladimir Putin. Ukrainian Prime-minister Azarov told journalists that the two presidents discussed about the 'preparation of a future treaty on strategic partnership' and that Yanukovych would visit Moscow on 17 December, when a 'major agreement' would be signed. The opposition accused the government on planning to seal a customs union agreement with Russia. Both Yanukovych and Putin denied this (Reuters 2013), however, the secrecy of their meeting maintained the speculations and fueled the protests.

On 10 December during an official visit in Ukraine, the EU's High Representative for Foreign Affairs, Catherine Aston, met with the protesters in the centre of Kiev. In the night of the same day, the police attacked the camp, which can be interpreted as a demonstration of the government that it was not willing to revert the decision of shifting its policy from the rapprochement with the EU towards better relations with Russia. (Lyubashenko 2014: 72).

On 17 December, President Yanukovych went on a state visit to Moscow, where he signed a series of agreements with his Russian counterpart, Vladimir Putin. Moscow promised Ukraine a loan of $15 billion and the reduction of gas prices from $400 to $268.5/tcm. This financial help should have been sufficient for Yanukovych until the presidential elections scheduled for March 2015. In addition, Russia eased a part of trade sanctions against Ukrainian exports, the two parts concluded a few agreements on production cooperation, essentially in the armament industry, and concurred to build a bridge over or a tunnel under the disputed Kerch Strait between Crimea peninsula and Russian mainland (Aslund 2015: 104). Vladimir Putin highlighted as well that 'this [help] does not come with any conditions attached and does not involve any increase, decrease or freeze of social welfare commitments, pensions, benefits and wages,' a clear allusion to the conditional aspects of the AA with the EU. He also gave assurances that the two presidents 'did not discuss at all today the question of Ukraine joining the Customs Union' (kremlin.ru 2013b). The Ukrainian opposition contested this agreement and vowed to continue the protests.

However, within the context of radicalization of the Euromaidan, the Ukrainian government was forced to make concessions to pro-EU supporters. On 28 January, prime-minister Azarov resigned and the 'dictatorial bills' were cancelled. As the situation became more complicated in Ukraine, immediately, on the night of 28/29 January, Russia tightened customs control for the Ukrainian exports and imposed a special additional customs duty for the owner of the goods (ЛІГАБізнесІнформ 2014). In addition, Moscow froze the delivery of the $15 billion loan, conditioning it of the formation of a new government.

On 6 February, Sergey Glazyev, a senior adviser to Russian President Putin declared in an interview for *Kommersant Ukraine* that the US was spending '$20 million weekly for funding, and weapons for the opposition and the rebels,' which was 'brutally interfering in the domestic affairs of Ukraine,' ignoring the 1994 Budapest Memorandum on Security Assurances. Glazyev warned that 'if Ukrainian authorities confront with a coup attempt, they will simply have no choice [but to use the force]' (Kommersant 2014). There is no evidence whether these declarations influenced Yanukovych to resort to force to restore order, however, on 7 February Ukrainian President had an informal meeting with Vladimir Putin in Sochi on the sidelines of the Winter Olympics. Neither side confirmed what they discussed (BBC 2014a), yet, shortly after, the Ukrainian authorities used force to disperse the protests.

On 18 February 2014, Yanukovych decided to restore order by escalating violence. 18 people were deadly shot by the police. Two days later snipers killed 80 people. The victims have become known as 'Heavenly Hundred' (Portnov and Portnova 2015: 69). These massacres determined 68 parliamentarians to leave Yanukovych's Party of the Regions, many of them starting fleeing the country. Meanwhile, the foreign ministers of Germany, France and Poland came to Kiev to mediate the negotiations between Yanukovych and the opposition parties. On 21 February, in the midst of the negotia-tions, Ukrainian president stated that he had to answer to a phone call from President Putin. After that conversation, Yanukovych made substantial concessions in negotiations and the security guards around the presidential administration and the Cabinet of Ministers withdrew. As Aslund (2015: 107–108) argues, the three EU foreign ministers got the impression that Putin had told Yanu-kovych to pack and leave.

The agreement concluded between Yanukovych and the op-position was stating *inter alia* that the president was to stay in power until the end of the year. However, after it was signed, on the same day, Ukrainian President left Kiev. Despite the video evidence that Ukrainian President packed his most valuable assets before leav-ing, Vladimir Putin related that Yanukovych left on 21 February to Kharkhov for a regional conference and did not have plans to flee the country. According to Putin, the Ukrainian leader called him from Kharkhov to ask to meet for consultations. However, because 'Yanukovych's life was in danger' and it was 'clear that in Ukraine it had been accomplished a coup d'etat,' Putin helped Yanukovych to flee to Russia, saving, thus, his life (see the documentary 'Cri-mea — the way back home,' sputniknews 2015). This scenario suited very well the Kremlin for explaining its further actions in Crimea.

Ukrainian parliament interpreted Yanukovych's absence as his *de facto* resignation, scheduled early presidential elections, and the speaker of parliament became the acting president of Ukraine. Both the EU and the US recognized the new authorities, Russia, however, refused to recognize the legality of Yanukovych's dismis-sal (Lyubashenko 2014: 82). After a week of absence, on 28 Febru-ary, Viktor Yanukovych appeared in a live conference in the Rus-sian city Rostov-on-Don and declared that in Kiev took place a coup d'etat, 'the power was sized by nationalist pro-fascists' and that he remained the legitimate president of Ukraine. Moreover, he asked Russia to intervene by military force in Ukraine, arguing that 'within the framework of the agreements Ukraine signed with Rus-sia, Russia has the authority to act and must act,' and he was 'sur-prised why Vladimir Putin was so restrained' (Yanukovych 2014).

It is to be mentioned that during the violent clashes of 18–21 February, Russian foreign minister accused the Western politicians to be responsible for the bloodshed and called them 'to put the interests of Ukraine and its people above their own geopolitical designs' (1tv.ru 2014a). Russian state-controlled media, besides reporting of anarchy, looting of military equipment by radicals, chaos and insecurity, announced that the Security Service of Ukraine had found out about secret negotiations of representatives of foreign states on a possible division of the country into several parts (1tv.ru 2014b). The stage for the annexation of Crimea was set.

As it happened in 2004 (during the 'Orange Revolution'), the Euromaidan (the name given to the 2013–2014 Ukrainian revolution) brought to power a pro-Western government. However, if after the 'Orange Revolution' Russia waited patiently the compromising of the Yushchenko-Timoshenko coalition, this time, the Kremlin sought to maintain its strategic positions in the Black Sea at any cost. Thus, already in the week of 14 February, when the tensions in Kiev were increasing, Vladislav Surkov, the personal adviser of Vladimir Putin, visited Crimea.

After the fled of Yanukovych to Russia, in Crimea, the pro-Russian parties started organizing anti-Maidan rallies. On 23 February the biggest rally gathered in Sevastopol an estimated 50,000 protesters. During the protest the local businessman and Russian citizen Alexey Chaliy was elected as 'mayor' and forced the governor of Sevastopol appointed by Kiev to leave (Shapovalova 2004: 254). On 26 February 2014, pro-Russian forces, military men without insignia, the so-called 'self-defence force,' started taking control of the peninsula. The next day they sized the Crimean parliament and the Council of Ministers buildings in Simferopol, raising the Russian flags. The occupation of the buildings did not meet resistance from the local police and the security guards. In the building occupied by the armed men, the local parliament held and emergency session during which it voted the dissolution of the government and the replacement of Crimean prime-minister Anatolii Mohyliov with Sergey Aksyonov, a member of Russian Unity Party that had won only 4% of the vote at the 2010 parliamentary elections. A referendum on the status of Crimea was scheduled for 25

May. During this session neither Mohyliov nor journalists were granted access into the parliament building, the local MPs had their phones confiscated and there was no possibility to verify whether the quorum was reached (Reuters 2014).

After the taking control of the local administration, the pro-Russian forces sized the Simferopol airport, the TV stations, other governmental buildings, established checkpoints on the border between the peninsula and the mainland Ukraine and isolated the local Ukrainian military bases from the headquarters. It has to be mention that the military men without insignia, the 'little green men,' sized the whole peninsula without firing a single shot, Ukrainian forces receiving orders not to open fire. Russia denied any involvement in the events in Crimea, suggesting that the Black Sea Fleet was neutral and its soldiers deployed at the military base were protecting the Fleet's possessions. Moscow implied that the 'little green men' were local 'self-defence forces' over whom Russia had no authority. However, in that period around 5,500–6,000 Russian soldiers together with their weapons had been transferred to Crimea from Russian Federation and the evidence showed that the units of the Russian army and the Crimean Self-Defence occupied the strategic infrastructure on the peninsula (Wilk 2014).

On 1 March, the new Crimean 'prime-minister,' Sergey Aksyonov called Russian President Putin 'to provide assistance in securing peace on the territory of the Autonomous Republic of Crimea' (BBC 2014b). The Kremlin did not answer to this request, however, on the same day, Russian parliament's upper house, the Federation Council, voted for the use of the armed forces of the Russian federation on the territory of Ukraine. Three days later, on 3 March, asked by Russian journalists whether Moscow was considering the accession of Crimea to Russia, Vladimir Putin rejected this option (Interfax 2014).

On 6 March 2014, the Crimean parliament voted to join the Russian Federation and added an explicit question about this on the voting form for referendum, rescheduled for 16 March. The next week Crimean deputies went further and adopted a declaration of independence.

On 16 March, Crimean population was asked within the referendum whether they wanted to reunite with Russia as a subject of the Federation and whether they wanted the restoration of the Crimean Constitution of 1992 and the preservation of the Crimea as part of Ukraine. According to Crimean and Russian official data 96.77% of the 83.1% of population that took part were in favour of joining Russia (RT 2014a). However, according to the Mejlis of the Crimean Tatar People, that boycotted the referendum, the percentage of those who voted on 16 March was between 30 and 40 (ukrinform.ua 2014), which correlated with the official results would mean that only 29%–38.7% of the Crimean population voted in favour of joining Russia.

The following day after the referendum, the Crimean parliament officially declared the independence of the Ukrainian peninsula, asked Moscow to admit it as a new subject of the Russian Federation with the status of a republic, made Russian ruble as the Crimea's official currency and announced that on 30 March the peninsula will switch to Moscow's time. On 18 March the Russian President Putin and the Crimean leaders signed the 'Agreement on the incorporation of the Republic of Crimea into the Russian Federation' (kremlin.ru 2014), that provided the establishment of two new federal subjects, the Republic of Crimea and Sevastopol as a city of federal importance. On 20 and 21 March the agreement was ratified by the State Duma and the Federation Council. On 21 March it was signed by president Putin, who officialised, thus the annexation of Crimea.

While the 'little green men' were occupying Crimea, in eastern Ukraine pro-Russian forces started demonstrations against the new government in Kiev. On 1 March around 7,000–10,000 people with Russian flags gathered in the centre of Donetsk. The wave of protest, fired for weeks by the alarmist reports in Russian and regional media about the radicalization of the Maidan, spread to other cities in eastern Ukraine. The manifestations were suspected of being sponsored by the former president Yanukovych, since the region used to be his fiefdom and his network of mayors and officialdome remained in place (Sakwa 2015: 148) after he fled to Russia.

In his 18 March 2014 speech, President Putin cynically addressed the people of Ukraine 'not [to] believe those who want [Ukrainians] to fear Russia, shouting that other regions will follow Crimea. [Russia] does not want to divide Ukraine; [Russia] does not need that' (Putin 2014a). However, as the events evolved in the eastern Ukraine with the occupation of the buildings of the local and regional administration, there appeared evidence of involvement of Russian military men in those events. As Sakwa (2015: 150) remarks, the buildings in Slavyansk were occupied not by 'self-defence' forces but by what appeared to be highly trained professional armed forces without insignia; while Gessen (2015) noted that the commandos had come from abroad, and that the people's uprising in Donbas became rather a covert invasion. The scholar also mentioned that the chief of the Slavyansk police assessed that the insurgents were not locals with hunting rifles but highly trained, well-armed men.

On 7 April 2014, the insurgents proclaimed the Donetsk People's Republic (DPR) and on 27 April, similarly, the pro-Russian activists proclaimed Lugansk People's Republic (LPR). The separatist leaders announced the creation of a 'People's Army' and scheduled referendums for 11 May to determine the future status of the region. As the insurgents continued to expand their territorial control by occupying government buildings in other cities across the regions of Donetsk and Lugansk, the Ukrainian government launched a counter-terrorist operation in the eastern Ukraine.

During the 17 April annual Direct Line, President Putin brought up into public debate the concept of Novorossiya. He recalled that Kharkov, Lugansk, Donetsk, Kherson, Nikolayev and Odessa were part of the region called Novorossiya back in the tsarist days and that even Russia lost these territories the people (Russians) remained there (Putin 2014b). Putin did not make any further suggestions concerning these regions, his intention being probably only to put more pressure on the Ukrainian government. On 24 May, DPR and LPR signed an agreement that established the 'Novorossiya Republic,' a step that was intended for the absorption of other regions of Ukraine into a pro-Russian separatist confederation. However, Novorossiya failed to achieve these objectives and in May 2015 the 'foreign minister' of DPR announced that the No-vorossia project had been put on hold because it did not fit into the Minsk cease-fire agreements signed by Putin as well (The Moscow Times 2015).

Within the context of Western sanctions on the annexation of Crimea, on 7 May 2014, Vladimir Putin publicly asked the pro-Russian separatists in Donetsk and Lugansk to postpone the referendums. However, the insurgents disregarded Putin's request and voted on 11 May for independence. The following day, the leader of 'People's militia', Igor Girkin, known as Strelkov, a former colonel in the Russian Army, proclaimed himself the 'Supreme Comander' of the DPR and declared outright war against Ukraine. Strelkov called also military assistance from Russia to fight against the 'genocide' unleashed by 'the Kiev junta' on the Donetsk population and because there was the 'threat of intervention by NATO' (Ukrainian Policy 2014). The Kremlin did not answer to this request.

NATO and western leaders have accused Russia several times of involvement in the conflict in the eastern Ukraine. Different reports were showing clearly the deployment of Russian service men in Donbas yet, despite the evidence, Moscow has refuted its involvement. However, like in the case of Crimea, when the Kremlin denied initially and then admitted its involvement in the events that led to the annexation of the Ukrainian peninsula, in December 2015, during his annual press conference, President Putin acknowledged that Russia had 'people there who deal with certain matters, including in the military area, but this does not mean that regular Russian troops are present there' (Putin 2015a). It was for the first time when the Kremlin admitted Russian presence in the eastern Ukraine.

The war in the eastern Ukraine varied in intensity. The violence escalated in May-June 2014, before Kiev signed the AA with the EU. Then the situation became even worse in July with the shooting down of Malaysia Airlines Flight MH17. While the Ukrainian government was accusing Russia and the pro-Russian insurgents for the killing of 298 people on board, Moscow was disseminating confusion about the event, suggesting that the civil plane was shot by Kiev military jets (RT 2014b). In August when it appeared that Ukrainian military offensive was closer to a victory, Russia deployed troops on Ukrainian border for military exercises. On 12 August, Moscow sent the first convoy of about 200 trucks with aid that crossed the border without Ukrainian permission. Meanwhile the insurgents succeeded in breaking out the encirclement and threatened to recover the lost positions. On 1 September, confronted with the accusations of invasion of Ukraine, President Putin answered president of the European Commission Jose Manuel Barroso that 'If I want to, I can take Kiev in two weeks' (The Telegraph 2014).

On 5 September 2014, in Minsk, the 'head of state' of DPR, Alexander Zakharchenko, and LPR 'prime minister' Igor Plotnitski, signed a cease-fire agreement with the former president Kuchma acting on behalf of the Ukrainian leadership. This occurred after the June 2014 secret meeting of American and Russian experts, including an ex-director of Russia's Foreign Intelligence Service and a top Russia advisor to George W. Bush on a Finnish island, where they discussed the crisis in Ukraine (The Atlantic 2014). The 12 points Minsk Protocol had been drafted by President Putin and agreed with President Poroshenko. It included *inter alia* the decentralisation of power to the Donetsk and Lugansk regions that would remain part of Ukraine.

The cease-fire agreement was violated already in the night of 6/7 September, however, for Russia the document was a great victory. It was for the first time the autonomous political agency of the rebels was recognized by Kiev, which meant that with about 10 per cent of its territory given special status, Ukraine's road to NATO membership was blocked (Sakwa 2015: 177).

January 2015 witnessed a new rise in violence that mobilized the leaders of Ukraine, Russia, France and Germany to conclude on 11 February 2015 a second Minsk cease-fire agreement. Violations of the Minsk II agreement have been registered as well, however, the number of casualties were greatly reduced and there were no changes in territorial control by the insurgents. This state of stalemate reminds the conflicts 'directed' by Rusia in the 1990s (in Transnistria, Abkhazia, South Ossetia, Nagorno-Karabakh) and suggests that most probable, Ukraine will join the 'community' of the former Soviet countries with 'frozen conflicts,' leaving Belarus the only EaP country without territorial problems.

Moscow keeps putting pressure on the government in Kiev and insists on the federalization of the former Soviet republic. Besides the pro-Russian separatism in Donbas, in spring-summer of 2015 Kiev was hinted that two other regions could follow the example of DPR and LPR. In May, the 'People's Rada of Bessarabia', claiming to represent several raions of the region of Odessa, called for autonomy of the region, and five months later proclaimed the Bessarabian republic of Budjak (Izvestiya 2015). Vzglyad (2015) 'recalled' in July that Transcarpathia was granted Ukraine by Stalin in 1945, but that it 'did not become fully "Ukrainian." The article highlighted that Transcarpathia is a distinctive region and Kiev's obstinacy to deny the possibility of federalization of the country, might determine the Transcarpathians to follow the example of Crimea and Donbas. These new separatist elements have not been too visible, however, they are signals that Russia can put more pressure on Kiev's government.

Kiev's relations with Moscow remain tense. Ukraine suspended any military cooperation with the neighbouring country and banned all direct flights to Russia. In September 2015 Crimean Tatar activists started a commercial blockade of the peninsula by preventing commercial trucks from entering Crimea. At the end of November, the annexed peninsula was cut off from its main source of electricity after a series of explosions damaged the pylons of the power lines that carry electricity to Crimea from mainland Ukraine. Five days later, Ukraine closed the airspace to all Russian planes, while Gazprom halted its gas exports to the former Soviet republic. In December 2015, Moscow threatened to take Ukraine to court if it did not repay a $3 billion Eurobond, taken out by the government of Yanukovych in December 2013.

The process of normalization of Ukraine-Russia relations will definitely not be easy. While President Poroshenko stated the three main conditions for the improvement of the relations with Moscow: the withdrawal of Russian forces from eastern Ukraine, the sealing of the border, and the return of Crimea; Moscow has insisted on 'special status' of Donetsk-Luhansk and has not shown any intentions to give up Crimea. Moreover, the relations between Kiev and Moscow got even worse in 2016, when Ukraine started implementing the DCFTA with the EU, despite Moscow's pressure for another delay[2]. In the December 2015 annual press conference, President Putin had already predicted the 'deterioration in [Russia-Ukraine] economic relations,' as Moscow would suspend Ukraine's membership of the CIS free trade zone. Russian president stated that the Kremlin would not impose any sanctions on Ukraine, but the fact that the former Soviet republic would not benefit from the privileges and preferences of the CIS free trade agreement, would mean an increase in trade tariffs between Russia and Ukraine from zero to a weighted average tariff of 6 per cent (Putin 2015a). On 1 January 2016, when the Ukraine-EU DCFTA took effect, Russia banned the import of Ukrainian agricultural products, raw materials and foodstuffs. In response, Kiev introduced import duties on Russian goods and banned the import of a series of commodity goods, including foodstuffs, chemical products and railway equipment (Unian 2016).

The case of Ukraine illustrates the most how far is Russia disposed to act in the former Soviet republics when its interests are at stake. The annexation of Crimea, the involvement in the war in Donbas, the pressure on the government of Kiev first not to sign then not to implement the AA with the EU are the most obvious violations of the sovereignty of a neighbouring independent country. However, despite the empirical evidence that incriminate Russia of not respecting the sovereignty and the territorial integrity of

---

2   Ukraine signed the DCFTA with the EU on 27 June 2014 and planned to implement it starting 1 November 2014. However, the Russian Federation expressed loud concerns about the negative effects on its economy and announced new tariffs on Ukrainian imports if the agreement entered into force in fall 2014. In September 2014 the EU, Ukraine and Russia had trilateral talks on the effects of the DCFTA and agreed to postpone its implementation until January 2016 in order "to avoid further destabilisation of the country and in particular to guarantee Ukraine's access to the CIS market under the Ukraine-Russia bilateral preferential regime" (http://ec.europa.eu/trade/policy/countries-and-regions/c ountries/ukraine/).

its neighbours, the Kremlin's discourse keeps insisting on the supremacy of sovereign rights of one country and inviolability of its borders. Within this context, the legitimate question that arises is how does Russia understand and interpret the concept of sovereignty in relation to its neighbours?

2.   Sovereignty from the Russian Perspective

The concept of sovereignty is one of the most controversial political notion of the contemporary international system (Shinoda 2000: 1). The huge body of literature on this concept shows both the great interest towards and the complexity of sovereignty in the contemporary world. There are many definitions of the concept, however, the common thread indicates a geopolitical character of sovereignty: a power exercised over a defined territory. Sovereignty has been defined, redefined, or divided into categories. One of the most complex analysis of the concept belongs to the American scholar Stephen Krasner who understands the term sovereignty as 'an institutional arrangement associated with a particular bundle of characteristics — recognition, territory, exclusive authority, and effective internal and transborder regulation or control' (Krasner 1999: 227). Based on these elements, Krasner explained the concept in four different ways: international legal (focused on the establishing the status of a political entity in the international system), Westphalian (based on the principles of the territoriality — the state exists in a specific territory; and the exclusion of external actors from domestic authority structures — within that territory the domestic political authorities are the sole arbiters of legitimate behavior), domestic (formal organization of political authority within the state and the ability of public authorities to exercise effective control within the borders of the state), and interdependence sovereignty (the ability of public authorities to regulate the flow of information, ideas, goods, people, pollutants, or capital across the borders of their state) (see Krasner 1999: 3–24).

Krasner's realist approach of the sovereignty suggests that the concept is very important and highly prized by states, however it is less a set of binding norms and more a convenient operating principle frequently violated in practice by powerful states (Ziegler 2012: 404). Hence, his characterization of the concept as organized hypocrisy.

While the realists understand the sovereignty as de facto power, the liberal internationalists suggest that sovereignty is the 'license from the international community to practice as an independent government in a particular territory' (Taylor 1999: 538), thus a rule-based concept, limited by global institutions. The realists also admit that the sovereignty is not unlimited and it can be constrained in the international arena, however, not by some systemic institutions but by other major powers within the logic of the balance of power (Ziegler 2012: 403).

The discourse of Russian political leaders suggest that Moscow has a realist approach towards the foreign policy and the concept of sovereignty. The sovereignty is seen as sacrosanct, and the Kremlin is insisting on the respect of this concept on international arena. In the interview given for the documentary 'Miroporiadok' (The World Order), broadcasted on *Rossiya TV* channel in December 2015, Vladimir Putin highlighted exactly the idea that the violation of sovereignty is the source of instability and chaos in the international arena. Russian President stressed that 'there should not be double or triple interpretation of sovereignty, and none should question whether the sovereignty of a state should be respected' (Putin 2015b). What one should keep in mind is that this declaration came within the context of the annexation of Crimea and Russian military involvement in the war in the eastern Ukraine. Thus, an analysis of Russia's perception of sovereignty is *sine qua non* for understanding Moscow's foreign policy in the 'near abroad.'

The Kremlin started manifesting a particular preoccupation for the concept of sovereignty after the 2004 Beslan terrorist attack. This event highlighted the deep-rooted insecurity about Russia's international position and domestic integrity and coincided with the improvement of the economic situation and political stabilization (Sakwa 2012: 13). The 'Orange Revolution' in Ukraine further deepened the anxiety of Moscow's political leadership about the internal and foreign security. Despite the efforts of the former Kremlin strategist Gleb Pavlovski, sent to Ukraine to 'manage' the elections in Kiev, the neighbouring country succeeded in installing a pro-Western government due to the strong resistance of the civil society. It was an outcome that raised fear in the Kremlin that Ukraine could play further the role of a Troyan Horse for the democratisation of Russia and that the West could export the 'color revolution' in Moscow. Russian political leaders perceived the 'Orange Revolution' as a 'special operation' of the West that managed the change of power in Kiev by the instrumentality of NGOs, and were seeking to prevent such a scenario in the Russian Federation.

In the spring of 2005, the First Deputy Head of the Presidential Administration, Vladislav Surkov, introduced in a speech about national priorities a new concept—'sovereign democracy' and in February 2006 presented the main elements of the concept in front of the members of Putin's party 'United Russia.' The sovereign democracy quickly became popular among Russian analysts and politicians and by the summer of 2006 the great majority of political class was solidarized around the concept. It was backed by the President Putin, even he seldom used it, and the biggest political party, 'United Russia,' established as a strategic objective in its political programme the 'qualitative renewal of the country as a sovereign democracy' (Orlov 2006).

The main idea of the sovereign democracy is that Russian is a democratic country, with a specific political culture and hence a distinctive view of sovereignty and democracy and that its domestic policy concerns only Russia and no external actor has any right to intervene in its internal affairs. Surkov (2006, 2009) argues that the consolidation of democracy in Russia should be based on its own pattern, that Russia alone would decide the 'democratic' rules it needs and would gradually implement structural reforms taking into account its historical and social features. He underlines that Russia is part of the European civilization but is a specific version of that civilization based on its national peculiarities. Surkov argues that Russian political culture is characterized by centralisation, personification, and idealisation; that comparing to the Western Eu-

rope in Russian 'intellectual and cultural practice synthesis pre-
dominates over analysis, idealism over pragmatism, imagery over
logic, intuition over rationality, the general over the particular'
(Surkov 2008: 12). Therefore, Russian politicians are seeking political wholeness through the centralisation of power functions, they
idealise the goals of political struggle and there is a personification
of political institutions. Surkov highlights that the centralisation of
the power, a strong executive, has played a positive role for Russian
sovereignty because it stabilised the society, prevented the
defragmentation of the country and supported the economic
growth. Thus, the centralisation of power is seen as necessary to
preserve the sovereignty and wholeness of Russia and to turn the
country from oligarchy towards democracy. In other words, Western version of democracy is not appropriate for Russia as it would
cost the country its social stability, in this respect Surkov bringing
the example of the beginning of 1990s when the West would have
encouraged the weakness of the state by imposing its version of democracy at the expense of social stability.

This interpretation of sovereignty is strongly embedded in
Westphalian tradition, which implies absolute authority over a
given people and territory and the right to exclude any external actor from possessing or exercising authority over a state's people
and territory (Ziegler 2012: 414). Even the concept sovereign democracy has not officially been assumed by Vladimir Putin, when
he talks about Russia's relations with the West, he often makes comments that fit exactly within its logic. In one of the most recent TV
interview Russian president drew attention that 'no one never
should impose to anyone any kind of values he considers right. We
have our own values, our own understanding of justice (…) This
concerns our traditional values, first of all our history, culture, traditions' (Putin 2015b), a clear reference to the West's critics on the
infringement of human rights and democracy in Russia and a critic
related to the recent revolutions in Ukraine and in the Arab world.

The Kremlin is, thus highlighting how much it prizes the sovereignty. However, there is not difficult to observe that in practice
there is a contradiction between Moscow's advocacy for this concept and its actions in the 'near abroad,' especially when we look at

the annexation of Crimea and Russia's military involvement in the destabilisation of eastern Ukraine. This approach betrays the hypocrisy of the states Krasner referred in his study on sovereignty. In other words, Moscow displays itself as a strong defender of Westphalian sovereignty as long it serves the Kremlin's interests (counteractive criticism about the breaches of Russian democracy and violation of human rights; the curtailing of spreading of Western democratic values; the centaralisation of the state, etc.) but does not refrain from violating the same Westphalian rules when it comes to its approach towards the former Soviet republics.

The concept of 'sovereign democracy' calls also for the democratisation of the international relations, which fits the neo-realist perspective of the international order based on the assumption that the international system is anarchic, formed by equal sovereign states (units), where 'none is entitled to command, none is required to obey' (Waltz 1979: 88). However, the units differ 'primarily by their greater or less capabilities for performing similar tasks' (Waltz 1979: 97). Thus, weaker states are not able to exercise sovereign control neither over their domestic nor foreign affairs and become dependent on stronger international actors. For Russia the status of great power is thus not only a matter of international prestige but rather a condition *sine qua non* for its status of true sovereignty.

Russia considers itself one of the truly sovereign countries in the world together with the USA, India and China, able and entitled to pursue an independent foreign policy, and capable to establish interest-based relations with other great powers of the system (Sakwa 2012:17). From Moscow's perspective, only a strong state can promote and defend its interests, the weaker states, however, are doomed to oscillate around the stronger one. The smaller states and multilateral organisations are seen as objects of great power diplomacy and the 'democratization of international relations' is seen as referring only to a group or 'Concert' of Great Powers, including Russia (Lo 2015: 42). Within this context, while Russia advocates for the principle of Westpahilan sovereignty and democratization of the international system where the units would benefit of formal equality, in practice it sees nothing wrong in limiting the sovereign rights of the weaker states, thus violating the principles it so strongly pleads for, especially when it comes to the 'near abroad.' This hypocritical approach of the concept of sovereignty has characterized Russia's relations with the former Soviet republics since the fall of the Soviet Union. These countries have not been seen by Russia as real sovereign international actors but as instrumental 'satellites' for regaining its status of a great power and of a pole in a multipolar world. As 'no great power ... walks alone' (Trenin 2007: 81).

Even after the annexation of Crimea, Moscow continued to advocate for national sovereignty and equality on international arena. The Kremlin has tried to cancel the discrepancy between the theory and practice through various arguments/strategies. Russia has denied any military involvement in Ukraine, portraying the conflict in eastern Ukraine as a civil war between the local Russian-speaking population and Kyiv. Moscow invoked the humanitarian intervention on behalf of Russian compatriots, which has been invoked not only in the case of Crimea but also in Abkhazia and South Ossetia (to this purpose Moscow has issued tens of thousands of passports to residents in neighbouring territories and countries); and Moscow has argued that Russia and Ukraine are not separate countries but have been intertwined for centuries (Lo 2015: 96, 107). The last argument has great implications for the reinterpretation of the rules of sovereignty. Since it implies that Ukraine is not a 'real' country, on the one side Russia's meddling in the affairs of Kiev is not portrayed as external interference but fraternal support and on the other side, Russia operates on the premise that international law applies only to properly independent entities, or Ukraine is an 'ahistorical' creation, like other former Soviet republics, and thus, they should have a different treatment (Lo 2015: 96). It is exactly the situation described by Krasner (1999) — organized hypocrisy, when a state violates the rules and interprets the sovereignty how it suits it better.

For Russia sovereignty remains a sacrosanct principle when it comes to its statehood, yet, it is interpreted in a different way when it comes to the former Soviet republics. The countries of the 'near abroad' are perceived as being too weak to be able to exercise sovereign control over their domestic or foreign affairs, therefore, they should remain dependent on the regional hegemon. However, how far Russia is willing to restrict the sovereignty of the former Soviet republics?

3.   Imperial ambitions?

The annexation of Crimea provided a powerful argument to the supporters of the thesis that Russia is seeking to physically re-create its former empire in the 'near abroad'. It was for the first time after the dissolution of the Soviet Union when Russia incorporated formally foreign territories. Moreover, the separatist war in Donbas and the 'resurrection' of the historical Novorossiya made the apologists of the idea of Russian traditional imperialist policy to assume that the southeast of Ukraine would face a similar scenario as Crimea. In addition to 'recovery' of Ukrainian territories, Russian neo-imperialists suggested that Moscow should start revising its borders with Belarus and Kazakhstan as well. The fever of 're-gathering of the land of Rus' seemed to be the new direction of Russian foreign policy. And yet, the political leadership has not confirmed a commitment to restoring the physical empire. The project Novorossiya had a short life and after the annexation of Crimea, Moscow refrained from incorporating any other territories despite the public requests of Donetsk and Lugansk Popular Republics and South Ossetia to join Russia. The question remains, however, how should we interpret Russia's foreign policy in the 'near abroad', in particular after the annexation of Crimea?

Before analyzing whether Russia's foreign policy in the 'near abroad' has an imperialist character, we should define the concept of empire first. There is a great body of academic literature on this topic and many interpretations of the concept. Traditionally, the empires have been seen as physical construction defined in narrow terms as the formal annexation of conquered territory, or in broader terms as any form of international economic inequality, as international power, as international exploitation and as international order (Doyle 1986: 20). The contemporary debates focused on two aspects of the empire: as a matter of formal sovereignty over annexed territories; and as informal domination, often by economic means.

Doyle combined the two aspects and defined empire as 'a relationship, formal or informal, in which one state controls the effective political sovereignty of another political society. It can be achieved by force, by political collaboration, by economic, social, or cultural dependence' (Doyle 1986: 45). This definition is, however, very broad and can easily include the policies of a great power or regional power under the umbrella of imperialism.

The thesis that Russia is pursuing an imperialist policy in the near abroad has been supported by a great number of specialists long before the recent events in Ukraine. Their arguments were based on the informal control of Moscow over the domestic and external politics of the former Soviet republics, which leaves a large margin of interpretation. However, the annexation of Crimea tilts the balance towards the supporters of the idea that Russia is a traditional imperialist power that seeks formal rule over the 'near abroad.' The case of Crimea is, indeed a strong argument for the latter. However, there is a number of counter-arguments to this thesis that challenge it.

In March 2014 it was for the first time after the dissolution of the Soviet Union when Russia annexed foreign territories. It did not happen during its economic pic or within a context of domestic debate on revision of borders (as it was in the beginning of 1990s). Many analysts asserted that the annexation of Ukrainian peninsula was part of Putin's strategy, who after having ensured the economic stability and the international prestige of the country in the first two mandates, was now looking for accomplishing the next stage of his plan — the restoration of former empire. However, besides Vladimir Putin's declarations that Russia is not seeking to restore the Soviet Union, his foreign policy has been the opposite of a land grabbing political leader. In fact, under president Putin Moscow gave up more Russian territory than any other leader except Lenin: in 2004 Russia achieved a definitive agreement with China over their border in exchange for the transfer of several major islands in the Ussuri River to Beijing's jurisdiction; in 2010 Moscow reached the agreement with Norway over the long contested maritime delineation of the Barents Sea. The two parts agreed to split down the middle, which turned out to advantage Norway, that received the bulk of the energy resources; also under Putin, Russia reached border agreements with Estonia and Latvia; in 2006 Moscow offered to return to the 1956 agreement with Japan and to return the two smallest of the four Kurile islands (about 6% of the disputed area) (Sakwa 2015: 116).

Thus, we would argue that Russia did not annex the Ukrainian peninsula for the sake of territorial expansion or imperial nostalgia. The decision to incorporate Crimea was determined first of all by security reasons. Sevastopol is hosting the Black Sea Fleet — Russia's biggest warm-water naval base, it has a strategic position that allows Moscow to project power in a Black Sea dominated by NATO countries, and defence Russia's southern borders. It is to be mentioned also that Sevastopol, besides being a naval base, has an extensive network of airfields, radar stations and ship repair yards, which have a strategic importance for Russia.

The Black Sea Fleet is Russia's best warm-water naval base. Moscow spent years trying to find an alternative to this port, including extending naval facilities at Novorosiisk and establishing basing rights in Abkhazia, however, there is no options that even begins to match Sevastopol (Sakwa 2015: 102). The Kharkov Pact (the so-called Fleet for gas agreement) signed in 2010 by Ukrainian president Yanukovych and Russian president Medvedev, extended the lease on Russian naval facilities in Crimea until 2042. However, it was fiercely criticized by the Ukrainian opposition, the politicians that had acceded to power after the Euromaidan. Within this context, the Kremlin feared that its naval base in Ukraine would be evicted (Sakwa 2015: 102) after the flight of Yanukovych.

The annexation of Crimea was motivated by the rationale of limiting NATO advancement to Russia's borders. Russia still perceives the North Atlantic Alliance as the main security threat and seeks to contain the advancement of the organisation in the 'near abroad'. The change in power in Kiev and with this the change in Ukrainian foreign policy orientation, that made the rapprochement with the EU its main priority, made the Kremlin anxious that this opened the door for Ukraine's accession to NATO. Even if during

the Euromaidan the issue of NATO was never mentioned and neither was it put into discussion by the new government in Kiev before the annexation of Crimea, Moscow was assuming that the expansion of Wider Europe would mandatory be accompanied by the
expansion of the North Atlantic alliance in the same countries.
These worries were fuelled by the fact that the vague promises
given to Georgia and Ukraine at the Bucharest NATO summit in
2008 were never revoked and by Moscow's assumption that the
rapprochement with the EU comes together with the rapprochement with NATO. The latter thesis was clearly expressed by Russian deputy prime minister Rogozin two months after the annexation of Crimea, when he warned Moldova that its neutral status will
change if it chose to join the EU, as before joining the EU, its members had joined NATO (Radio Free Europe Radio Liberty 2014).

On the other side, the AA *per se* with the EU, Ukraine was determined to sign, did not please Russia. Besides the economic provisions and the requirements to adopt a large part of the EU's *acquis
communautaire*, the agreement provides also 'gradual convergence
in the area of foreign and security policy, including the Common
Security and Defence Policy (CSDP)' (Art. 7.1) and military-techno-
logical cooperation (Art. 10.3), which meant that once Ukraine
signed the AA, the EU was to assert exclusivity in secure matters.
However, 22 out of 28 EU member states are also NATO members
and the Ukrainian border is at about 500 kilometres from Moscow.
Thus, the whole issue of EU-Ukraine AA acquired an existential
character for Russia (Sakwa 2015: 75) that saw in the annexation of
Crimea the solution for securing its borders and stances in the Black
Sea.

That security issue was the main reason behind the annexation
of Crimea was also acknowledged by President Putin during his
address of 18 March 2014: 'we have already heard declarations from
Kiev about Ukraine soon joining NATO [...] It would have meant
that NATO's navy would be right there in this city of Russia's military glory, and this would create not an illusory but a perfectly real
threat to the whole of southern Russia' (Putin 2014a); and confirmed later more explicitly: 'we could not allow our access
to the Black Sea to be significantly limited; we could not allow

NATO forces to eventually come to the land of Crimea and Sevastopol [...] and cardinally change the balance of forces in the Black Sea area' (Putin 2014c).

Another counterargument to the thesis of Russian formal imperialism is linked to the costs of integration of new territories. Financing Crimea, including pensions payment is estimated to cost Russia $6–7 billion a year. This budget is comparable to that of Krasnodar region — which has double population and triple surface area. Only in the first three months after the annexation of Ukrainian peninsula it cost the federal budget over $1 billion excluding the pension payments. Besides these expenses, Russia will have to support the much bigger costs of infrastructure projects the peninsula needs in order to get linked with Russia: the Kerch Strait bridge, systems for water and electricity supply, whose total expenses may reach $30 billion (Zubarevich 2015: 53).

Even during the periods of economic prosperity these costs were not to be neglected, however, they are more felt in the current situation. Russia is crossing one of the deepest financial crisis and economic recession. At the end of 2014 the ruble lost more than 40% against the dollar and its value continued to drop reaching the ratio of 82 rubles per US dollar in January 2016, comparing to 35 rubles per US dollar in January 2014. Russian economy shrank 3.8 per cent in 2015 (Reuters 2016). These negative economic evolutions were caused by the fall in price of oil but also by the economic sanctions the West imposed against Russia over the annexation of Crimea and the military involvement in the war in Donbas.

To integrate Crimea with the mainland Russia, Moscow had to redirect the state budget funds from other investment projects. Thus, in May 2014 the government announced that suspended the construction of Taman port in Krasnodar region and the bridge over the Lena River in Yakutia and that the funds would be reallocated to the upgrade of infrastructure in Crimea (Tass 2014). The financial burden is clearly high and the opinion polls in Russia shows a growing in the number of those who begin to question whether the annexation of Crimea was in the country's interests (Russia Beyond the Headlines 2014).

The incorporation of Ukrainian peninsula has cost Moscow dearly on international arena as well. Russia's membership to G8 has been suspended, the Parliamentary Assembly of the Council of Europe has deprived Russia of voting rights, the negotiations with the EU on the new Partnership and Cooperation Agreement and the talks on visas have been suspended, as well as all practical co-operation with NATO. Beyond the international isolation, the economic sanctions of the West had a strong economic impact on Russian economy, especially by restricting the financial availability for Russia from external markets.

As one can notice, the thesis of Russian formal imperialism in the 'near abroad' is not logic for Russia, despite the 2014 land grab. The annexation of Crimea could rather fit into the logic of pragmatism if we consider Selezneva's definition of this concept – 'a way of making short-term decisions, grasping opportunities to achieve practical results, without considering the long-term consequences and, in some cases, even the morality of the decisions' (Selezneva 2002: 10). In fact Moscow took advantage of political instability and the weakness of central administration in Kiev to secure its strategic positions in the Black Sea; most probably did not anticipate the extent of consequences; and disregarded the morality of violations of a series of international treaties, starting with the 1975 Helsinki Final Act of the Conference on Security and Co-operation in Europe, breaching the territorial integrity of a neighbouring country it committed to defend through the 1994 Budapest Memorandum.

However, the pragmatism cannot explain the general trend of Russia's policy in the 'near abroad'. It could be admitted in the case of Crimea and has logic from the perspective of political discourse about the EEU, for instance, that imply that the union's goal is to unite the former Soviet countries and resources for development in their common interest, allowing thus 'each of its members more quickly and in a stronger position to integrate into Europe' (Putin 2011). However, the rush of integrating Armenia into the EEU contradicts the logic of pragmatism. The country is poor, does not represent any economic gain for the EEU and brings territorial conflict to the union. In addition, Armenia does not even have a common border with the EEU. Neither the concept of spheres of influence, called formally by president Medvedev 'spheres of privileged interests', fits the logic of pragmatic approach towards the 'near abroad'. Defined as 'a determinate region within which a single external power exerts a predominant influence, which limits the independence of freedom of action of political entities within it' (Keal, 1983: 15), a sphere of influence could be seen rather as a characteristic of informal imperialism.

The informal imperialism is a very broad concept, it refers to informal domination, which can be achieved often by economic means, but also by political collaboration, and social, or cultural dependence. This would easily fit under the umbrella of imperialism not only Russia's relations with the 'near abroad', but also the British Commonwealth, the Organisation of Farncophonie, US or China's foreign policies. On the other side the annexation of Crimea does not make much sense within the logic of informal imperialism. It would have been enough to create a secessionist protracted conflict in the Ukrainian peninsula in order to exercise indirect control of the region and on Ukrainian government on the whole, instead of land grab that implies a great responsibility both domestically and internationally.

One could not deny that Russian foreign policy has imperialist elements, however, these should rather be explained by the fact that with the physical disappearance of the empire the features established in the imperial period did not suddenly all disappear. Russia goes through a post-imperial period and still has a sense of entitlement toward the former Soviet republics that arises from the perception of a shared history, civilization and language, as well as strategic imperatives (Lo 2015: 102). It takes generations to change ideas and it happened with other former empires as well. Writing about Russia's post-imperialism, Trenin (2011: 25) make a comparison with British and French Empires and argues that even their physical form disappeared long before the dissolution of the Soviet Union, in a way neither Britain nor France is completely out of its imperial phase.

As we have argued, Russia is locked in the realist worldview, based on concepts of balance of power and zero-sum games. If we analyse the annexation of Crimea within this context, Russia's land grab appears more logic. The arguments of the Kremlin suggest that Moscow has annexed Crimea for limiting the expansion of the Western bloc towards Russia's borders. These arguments fit the logic of balance of power, as well as Moscow's foreign policy in the near abroad', based on controlling the smaller former Soviet republics — domination for the sake of international position and containment of rival power. Russia undermines the rapprochement of the former Soviet republics to the EU in order to prevent their integration into the West's security system and strongly opposes to the advancement of NATO into the 'near abroad'. The Kremlin 'warned' the North-Atlantic Organisation in 2008 in Georgia and increased its assertiveness in Crimea in 2014. Furthermore, the involvement in Donbas is determined also by the rationale of limitation of NATO advancement in the region. Aware that the West and Ukraine might have accepted in the end the loss of Crimea, the former Soviet country standing great chance to be included in West's security architecture, the Kremlin has supported the conflict in Donbas in order to keep its neighbour away from NATO. However, while the insurgents called for independence and unification with Russia on the model of Crimea, Moscow advocated a federalization of Ukraine and devolution of significant constitutional powers to Donetsk and Lugansk regions. This would allow Russia to leverage the threat of the possible secession of these regions in future and rule out Ukrainian membership in NATO or the EU for decades (Lo 2015: 111). In fact, neither the EU nor NATO is willing to import instability into their framework and a federative status of the neighbouring country would allow Donetsk and Lugansk, controlled by Russia, to block any foreign policy decision of Kiev.

On the other side, neither the EEU is motivated by imperial rationale but by the same logic of limiting the influence of the West in the 'near abroad' and preventing the rival bloc's hegemony in world economy.

Conclusions

At the beginning of the EaP Moscow, 'tolerated' rapprochement of former Soviet republics with the EU. It was convinced, probably, that – in the absence of an EU membership perspectives – these states would sooner or later 'get bored' with the European initiative. Or it assumed that the EaP would imply a sort of splitting of influence in the EU' and Russia's common neighbourhood: the former Soviet republics would join the liberal democratic and economic regime of the West; however, at the same time, they would acquiesce, in the hard security sphere, to continuing influence of their hegemonic neighbour (see Emerson 2009). The prospects of an initialling or even signing of the Association Agreements with the EU at the 2013 Vilnius summit and the security implications of this treaty determined Moscow to reshape its approach and policy. Russia saw in these agreements the 'danger' of an advancement of the Western security bloc towards its borders. Armenia's September 2013 decision to suspend negotiations of its Association Agreement with the EU and to join instead the future EEU was perceived by the Kremlin as a great geopolitical victory, and it thus tried to apply a similar formula to Kiev. However, its tactics in Ukraine proved to be catastrophic. Instead of keeping Kiev in its orbit by convincing Yanukovych to suspend the signing of the AA with the EU, Russia propelled a revolution.

Losing its influence in Kiev, confronted with a 'derailment' of the second biggest Slavic former Soviet republic towards the West and a possible NATO advancement to its borders, Moscow acted ruthlessly. It annexed Crimea and tried to destabilize Ukraine through a secessionist war in the Donbas as well as economic pressure. These actions were less motivated by imperial nostalgia than by the rationale of containing the advancement of West's security system to its borders. It was the first time that the Russian Federation annexed a foreign territory, but not the first time when it used the separatist card in neigbouring countries.

Russia has used threats to territorial integrity in all of the countries of the European 'near abroad'. Armenia and Azerbaijan have been played with Nagorno Karabakh. In Georgia, after recognizing the independence of Abkhazia and South Ossetia, the Kremlin put more pressure on Tbilisi by signing with the two breakaway regions comprehensive alliance agreements. Tiny Moldova was threatened with, besides Transnistria, two more possible secessionist conflicts in the North and South of the country. Finally, Belarus has been 'reminded' unofficially that its eastern provinces were granted by Russia. Yet, these signals and policies should not be read as stages in the implementation of a plan to rebuild the empire.

Economic leverage and the projection of hard power have been used successfully as well. However, all these tactics were aimed not at keeping these countries close in order to re-integrate them in a new empire but to keep them closer in order to prevent further advancement of the 'adverse' Western bloc into the 'near abroad' and to counterbalance the West's influence in the international system. This was and is consistent with the zero-sum mentality of Russian political leaders and follows from the Kremlin's realist worldview that perceives countries in its immediate neighbourhood as both, a security shield against NATO and the West, as well as satellite actors enhancing Moscow's international prestige vis-à-vis other poles of the multipolar international system.

References

1tv.ru (2013a), 'В Киеве сторонники оппозиции проводят митинги против сворачивания сближения с ЕС' [In Kiev, opposition supporters hold rallies against the shifting from the rapprochement with the EU], 24 November, available online at: http://www.1tv.r u/news/world/246847.

1tv.ru (2013b), 'Глава дипломатии Евросоюза второй раз за последние сутки встречается с представителями оппозиции' [The head of EU diplomacy, meets the second time in recent days with the representatives of the opposition], 11 December, available online at: http://www.1tv.ru/news/world/248111.

1tv.ru (2014a), 'На Украине в антитеррористической операции могут быть задействованы военные' [In Ukraine, in the anti-terrorist operation may be involved military], 19 February, available online at: http://www.1tv.ru/news/world/252608.

1tv.ru (2014b), 'По многим регионам Украины прошла волна беспорядков,' [In many regions of Ukraine has been a wave of unrest], available online at: http://www.1tv.ru/news/world /252738.

Adomelt, Hannes (2011), 'Russia's 'Partnerships for Modernization': origins, content and prospects', *The EU-Russia Center review*, issue 19, October.

Andréani, Jacques (2008), 'The reasons Europe has so disappointed Putin's Russia', *Europe's World*, pp. 31–35.

Association Agreement between the European Union and its Member States, of the one part, and Ukraine, of the other part (2014), L161/1, Official Journal of the European Union, 29 May, available online at: http://eeas.europa.eu/ukraine/docs/association_agreement_ukraine_2014_en.pdf.

Avere, Derek (2009), 'Competing rationalities: Russia, the EU and the 'shared neighbourhood'', *Europe-Asia Studies*, vol. 61, no.10.

Averyano-Minskii, Kirill (2015), quoted in 'Русские националисты ставят под сомнение целостность Беларуси' [Russian nationalists questions the integrity of Belarus], in Belarusskii Partizan, 15 March, available online at: http://www.belaruspartisan.org/politic/298576/.

Baev, Pavel K. (2008a), 'From West to South to North: Russia Engages and Challenges Its Neighbours', *International Journal*, Vol. 63, No. 2, Russian Resurgence, Spring, pp. 291–305.

Baev, Pavel K. (2008b) Russian energy policy and military power. Putin's quest for greatness, Routledge.

Barysh, Katinka (2010), 'The EU-Russia Partnership for Modernization', The EU-Russia center review, *Issue 15*, October.

Barysh, Katinka; Cocker, Christopher; Jesien, Leszek (2011), *EU-Russia relations. Time for a realistic turnaround*, Centre for European Studies, Brussels.

BBC (2013), 'Ukrainians rally over government's snub to EU', 22 November, available at: http://www.bbc.com/news/world-europe-25050202.

BBC (2014), 'Russia's Sergey Lavrov: Ukraine getting 'out of control', 21 January, available at: http://www.bbc.com/news/world-europe-25823091.

BBC (2014a), 'Putin meets Ukraine's Yanukovych on Sochi sidelines,' 8 February, available online at: http://www.bbc.com/news/world-europe-26096362.

BBC (2014b), 'Ukraine crisis: Crimea leader appeals to Putin for help,' 1 March, available online at: http://www.bbc.com/news/world-europe-26397323.

BBC (2015), 'The great Moldovan bank robbery', 18 June, available online at: http://www.bbc.com/news/magazine-33166383.

Beachain, Donacha O. and Polese, Abel (2010) *The colour revolutions in the former Soviet republics. Successes and failures*, Routledge.

Benes, Karoly (2009), 'European Council endorses Eastern Partnership', *Central Asia Caucasus Analyst*, May 26, available online at http://www.cacianalyst.org/?q=node/5074.

Birov, Eduard (2015), 'Минску пора определяться' [Minsk has to make its choice], in Vzglyad, 7 April, available online at: http://vz.ru/opinions/2015/4/7/738010.html.

Bloomberg (2013), 'Yanukovych Defends Ukraine EU Trade Pact as Competitiveness Lags,' 6 November, available online at: http://www.bloomberg.com/news/articles/2013-11-06/yanukovych-defends-ukraine-eu-trade-pact-as-competitiveness-lags.

Bosse, Giselle (2011), 'The EU's relations with Moldova: Governance, partnership or ignorance?', *Europe-Asia Studies*, 62:8, pp. 1291–1309.

Bova, Russell (2010), 'Russia and Europe after the Cold War: cultural convergence or civilizational clash?', in Engelbrekt, Kjell and Nygren, Bertil (eds.), *Russia and Europe. Building bridges, digging trenches*, Routledge, pp. 19–39.

Brown, Archie (2009) 'Forms without substance', *Journal of Democracy*, Volume 20, Number 2, April, pp. 47–51.

Cameron, Fraser (2007), *An introduction to European foreign policy*, Routledge Taylor and Francis Group, London and New York.

Casier, Tom (2007) 'The clash of integration process? The shadow effect of the enlarged EU on its Eastern neighbours', in Malfliet, Katlijn; Verpoest, Lien and Vinokurov, Evgeny (eds.), *The CIS, the EU and Russia. The challenges of integration*, Palgrave Macmillan.

Casier, Tom (2011), 'The Rise of Energy to the Top of the EU-Russia Agenda: From interdependence to Dependence?', *Geopolitics*, 16:3, pp. 536–552.

Cecire, Michael (2015), 'Divide and Conquer In Georgia. How Russia Is Turning the Country Against Itself,' in *Foreign Affairs*, 10 November, available online at: https://www.foreignaffairs.com/articles/georgia/2015-11-10/divide-and-conquer-georgia.

Celeste, Wallander (2005), 'The challenge of Russia for U.S. policy', *Testimony before the Committee on Foreign Relations United State Senate*, 21 June, available online at: http://csis.org/testimony/challenge-russia-us-policy.

Chambers, Luke (2010), 'Authoritarianism and foreign policy: the twin pillars of resurgent Russia', *Caucasus Review of International Affairs*, Vol. 4, Issue 2, available online at: http://cria-online.org/11_3.html.

Cianciara, Agnieszka K. (2009), 'The Union for the Mediterranean and the Eastern partnership: perspectives from Poland, Czech Republic and Hungary', Report of the Institute of Public Affairs.

Civil.ge (2012), 'Videos of Inmates Abuse, Rape Emerge,' 19 September, available online at: http://www.civil.ge/eng/article.php?id=25220.

Common Strategy of the European Union on Russia (1999/414/CFSP).

Concept of the Foreign Policy of the Russian Federation [Концепция внешней политики Российской Федерации], approved by President of the Russian Federation V. Putin on 12 February 2013.

Council of the European Union (2009), 'Joint Declaration of the Prague Eastern Partnership Summit', Brussels, May 7, 8435/09 (Presse 78).

Cwieck-Kaprovicz Jaroslaw (2010), 'Russia's vision of relations with the European Union', *Bulletin* nr. 82, May, The Polish Institute of International Affairs.

Debardeleben, Joan (2009) 'The impact of EU enlargement on the EU-Russian relationship', in Kanet, Roger E. (ed.), *Resurgent Russia and the West: the European Union, NATO and beyond*, Dordrecht 2009.

Deschide.md (2014), 'Întâlnire secretă la Bălți. Ce lovitură pregătește Furmuzal' [Secret meeting in Balti. What prepares Formuzal], 10 June, available online at: http://deschide.md/ro/news/politic/217 7/SURSE--Întâlnire-SECRETĂ-la-Bălți-Ce-lovitură-pregătește-Form uzal.htm.

Donaldson, Robert H. and Nogee, Joseph L. (2009), *The foreign policy of Russia. Changing systems, enduring interests*, Ed. M.E. Sharpe, New York.

Doyle, Michael W. (1986), *Empires*, Cornell University Press, Ithaca and London.

DW (2014), 'Ukraine, Georgia and Moldova sign deals strengthening political, trade ties to EU,' 27 June, available online at: http://ww w.dw.com/en/ukraine-georgia-and-moldova-sign-deals-strengthen ing-political-trade-ties-to-eu/a-17741114.

E-Democracy (2009), 'Medvedev about Chisinau's conduct over protesters', available online at: http://www.e-democracy.md/en/elect ions/parliamentary/2009/electoral-news/20090409/#c7.

Economist Intelligent Unit, 'Democracy Index 2011', *The Economist*, 2011, available online at: http://www.eiu.com/Handlers/WhitepaperH andler.ashx?fi=Democracy_Index_Final_Dec_2011.pdf&mode=wp

Emerson, Michael (2009), 'Do we detect some neo-Finlandisation in the Eastern neighbourhood?' CEPS Commentary, 28 May, available at: https://www.ceps.eu/publications/do-we-detect-some-neo-finlan-disationeastern-neighbourhood.

Emerson, Michael (2010), 'Russia in Europe and the West', April, Centre for European Policy Studies, available online at: http://www.ceps.e u/book/russia-europe-and-west.

Euractiv (2015), 'US, Russia and EU should work together to combat ISIS, says Juncker', 19 November, available at: http://www.eur activ.com/sections/global-europe/juncker-usa-russia-and-eu-shoul d-work-togethercombat-isis-319635.

European Consensus on Development (1996), 'Joint statement by the Council and the representatives of the governments of the Member States meeting with the Council, the European parliament and the Commission (2006/C 46/01)', *Official Journal of the European Union*, C 46/1, 24. 2. 2006.

Eyl-Mazzega, Marc-Antoine (2010), 'Les relations entre l'Union Europeene et la Russie: l'amorce d'un parteneriat de raison?', January, available online at: www.ceri-sciences-po.org.

Financial Times (2015), 'Georgia wary of Moscow deals with South Ossetia and Abkhazia,' 18 February, available online at: http://www.ft.co m/intl/cms/s/0/cfa4e440-b78c-11e4-8807-00144feab7de.html#axzz 3tk6ywmZq.

Forsberg, Tuomas and Herd, Graeme P. (2005) 'The EU, human rights and the Russo-Chechen conflict', *Political Science Quarterly*, Vol. 120, No. 3, pp. 455–478.

Gessen, Keith (2015), 'Why not kill them all?' in London Review of Books, vol. 36, nr. 17, 11 September, pp. 18–22.

Goble, Paul (2014), 'Who is behind the new Talysh-language TV broadcass in Azerbaijan?' in Eurasia Daily Monitor, Vol. 11, Issue 2019, 9 December.

Goldman, Marshall I. (2010) *Petrostate. Putin, power and the new Russia*, Oxford University Press.

Götz, Elias (2015), 'It's geopolitics, stupid: explaining Russia's Ukraine policy', Global Affairs, 1:1, pp. 3–10.

Grachev, Andrei (2005) 'Putin's foreign policy choices', in, Pravda, Alex (ed.), *Leading Russia: Putin in perspective*, Oxford University Press.

Gvosdev, Nikolas K. and Marsh, Christopher (2014), *Russian Foreign Policy. Interests, Vectors, and Sectors*, Sage, CQPress, Los Angeles, London, New Delhi, Singapore, Washington DC.

Haas de, Marcel (2009), 'Medvedev's Security policy: a provisional assessment', *Russian analytical digest*, nr. 62, June.

Haukkala, Hiski (2010), The EU-Russia strategic partnership. The limits of post-sovereignty in international relations, Routledge.

Herd, Graeme P. (2009) 'Russia's sovereign democracy: instrumentalization, interests and identity', in Kanet, E. Roger (ed.), *A resurgent Russia and the West: the European Union, NATO and beyond*, Dordrecht.

Hettne, B. and Söderbaum, F. (2005), 'Civilian Power or Soft Imperialism? The EU as a Global Actor and the Role of Interregionalism', *European Foreign Affairs Review* 10, pp. 535–52.

Hill, Cristopher and Smith, Michael (2005), *International Relations and the European Union*, Oxford University Press.

Hopf, Ted. (2008) *Russia's European choice*, Palgrave Macmillan.

House of Lords (2014), Corrected transcript of evidence taken before the Select Committee on the European Union, External Affairs (Sub-Committee C), inquiry on "The EU and Russia', Evidence Session No. 1, 10 July, London.

House of Lords (2015), European Union Committee 6th Report of Session 2014-15, 'The EU and Russia: before and beyond the crisis in Ukraine', 10 February, London.

Independent (2015), 'Lukaşenko avertizează Moscova: Sunt gata să înarmez jumătate de milion de belaruşi' [Lukashenko warns Moscow: I am ready to arm half a million Belarusians], 29 April, available online at: http://independent.md/lukasenko-avertizeaza-moscova-sunt-gata-sa-inarmez-jumatate-de-milion-de-belarusi/#.V mVkPEsrRlK.

Interfax (2014), 'Россия не рассматривает вариант присоединения Крыма к России' [Russia is not considering the option of accession of Crimea to Russia], 4 March, available online at: http://www.inter fax.ru/russia/362633.

Izvestiya (2015), 'В Бессарабии хотят провести референдум о самоопределении' [Bessarabia wants to hold a referendum on self-determination], 29 October, available online at: http://izvesti a.ru/news/594128.

Jackson, Robert and Sørensen, Georg (2003), *Introduction to international relations. Theories and approaches*, Oxford University Press Inc., New York.

Johnson, David (2009), 'A Problem with the Udder. Belarus and Russia Are Tumbling into a Full-Blown Trade War That Can Have Only One Outcome,' in Johnson's Russia List, available online at: http://ww w.russialist.org/archives/2009-108-37.php.

Kanet, Roger E. (2007), *Russia. Re-emerging great power*, Palgrave Macmillan.

Kanet, Roger E. (2009) *A resurgent Russia and the West: the European Union, NATO and beyond*, Dordrecht.

Karagiannis, Emmanuel (2012), 'The 2008 Russian–Georgian war via the lens of Offensive Realism', *European Security*, pp. 1–20.

Kavkaz online (2013), 'Армения может войти в состав России' [Armenia may join Russia], 7 May, available online at: http://kavkasia.net/Ar menia/article/1367954802.php.

Keal, Paul (1983), *Unspoken rules and superpower Dominance*, London, Mcmillan.

Keohane, Robert O (1986), 'Reciprocity in international relations', *International Organization*, Vol. 40, no. 1, pp. 1–27.

Keohane, Robert O. (1989), *International institutions and state power: essays in international relations theory*, Boulder, CO: Westview Press.

Keohane, Robert O. and Hoffmann, S. (eds.) (1993), *After the Cold War: international institutions and state strategies in Europe, 1989–1991*, Cambridge, MA, Harvard University Press.

Keukeleire, Stephan and MacNaughtan, Jennifer (2008), *The foreign policy of the European Union*, Palgrave Macmillan.

Kiselyov, Dmitri (2013), 'Украина и евроинтеграция. Украинская оппозиция собирает майдан' [Ukraine and the European integration. Ukrainian opposition gathers maidan], 24 November, available online at: http://vesti7.ru/news?id=41744.

Kobrinskaya, Irina (2007), 'The post-Soviet space: from the USSR to the Commonwealth of Independent States and beyond', in Malfliet, Katlijn; Verpoest, Lien and Vinokurov, Evgeny (eds.), *The CIS, the EU and Russia. The challenges of integration*, Palgrave Macmillan

Kobrinskaya, Irina (2009), 'Russia and the European Union. A keystone relationship', *Documentos Cidob Europa 6*, Ed. Cidob, Barcelona.

Kokoshin, A. (2006), *Real'nyi suverenitet v sovremennoi miropoliticheskoi sistemy*, [Real sovereignty in world political system], 3rd edition, Moscow, Evropa.

Kommersant (2009), Interview with V. Voronin, ""Восточное партнерство" напоминает кольцо вокруг России" [The Eastern Partnership remembers a circle around Russia], February 27, available online at: http://kommersant.ru/doc/1126593.

Kommersant (2014), 'Сергей Глазьев: федерализация — уже не идея, а очевидная необходимость' [Sergei Glazyev: federalization - is no longer an idea, but a clear need], 6 February, available online at: http://www.kommersant.ru/doc/2400532.

Kommersant.ru (2013), 'Чтобы попасть в Евросоюз, украинская оппозиция пошла по знакомому адресу' [To get into the EU, the Ukrainian opposition went on the familiar scenario], 25 November, available online at: http://www.kommersant.ru/doc/2351846.

Kontzeptziya vneshney politiki Rossisyskoy Federatzyi [The Foreign Policy Concept of the Russian Federation] (1999).

Korosteleva, Elena (2011b), 'The Eastern Partnership initiative: a new opportunity for neighbours?', *Journal of Communist Studies and Transition Politics* 27:1, pp. 1–21.

Korosteleva, Elena A. (2011a), 'Change or Continuity: Is the Eastern Partnership an Adequate Tool for the European Neighbourhood?', *International Relations* 25 (2), pp. 243–262.

Kozyrev, Andrei (1992) 'Russia: a chance for survival', *Foreign Affairs*, Vol. 71, No. 2, pp. 1–16.

Krasner, Stephen D. (1999), *Sovereignty: Organized Hypocrisy*, Princeton University Press, Princeton, New Jersey.

Krastev, Ivan (2007), 'Russia vs Europe: the sovereignty wars', September 5, available online at: http://www.opendemocracy.net/article/russia_vs_europe_the_sovereignty_wars.

Krastev, Ivan (2008), 'The EU, Russia and the crisis of the post-Cold War European order', *Europe's World*, available online at: http://www.eu ropesworld.org/EWSettings/%20Article/tabid/191/ArticleType/a rticleview/ArticleID/20551/Default.aspx.

Kremlin.ru (2013a), 'Press statements following Russian-Armenian talks,' 3 September, available online at: http://en.kremlin.ru/event s/president/transcripts/19142.

Kremlin.ru (2013b), 'Press statement following a meeting of Russian-Ukrainian Interstate Commission,' 17 December, available online at: http://en.kremlin.ru/events/president/transcripts/19854.

Kremlin.ru (2014), 'Договор между Российской Федерацией и Республикой Крым о принятии в Российскую Федерацию Республики Крым и образовании в составе Российской Федерации новых субъектов' [The agreement between the Russian Federation and the Republic of Crimea on incorporation of the Republic of Crimea into the Russian Federation and the establishment of new subjects of the Russian Federation], 18 March, available online at: http://www.kremlin.ru/events/president/news/20605.

Kulhanek, Jakub (2010), 'The fundamentals of Russia's EU policy', *Problems of Post-Communism*, vol. 57, no. 5, September/October, pp. 51–63.

Kyiv Post (2010), 'Yanukovych: Ukraine will remain a neutral state,' 7 January, available online at: https://web.archive.org/web/20100121 145322/http://www.kyivpost.com/news/politics/detail/56539.

Leonard, Marc and Popescu, Nicu (2007), 'A power audit of EU-Russia relations', European Council of Foreign Relations, November.

Leonard, Mark and Popescu, Nicu (2008) 'A five-point strategy for EU-Russia relations', *Europe's World*, Spring, pp. 20–24

Levitsky, Steven and Way, Lucan A. (2006), 'Linkage versus leverage. Rethinking the international dimension of the regime change', *Comparative politics*, Vol. 38, nr. 4 July, pp. 379–400.

Light, Margot (2001), 'The European Union's Russian foreign policy', in Malfliet, Katlijn; Verpoest, Lien, *Russia and Europe in a changing international environment*, Leuven University Press.

Lo, Bobo (2003), *Vladimir Putin and the evolution of Russian foreign policy*, The royal Institute of international Affairs, Blackell Publishing.

Lo, Bobo (2015), *Russia and the new world disorder*, Chatham House, Brookings Institute Press, London and Washington.

Lynch, Allen C. (2001), 'The Realism of Russia's Foreign Policy', *Europe-Asia Studies*, Vol. 53, Issue 1, pp. 7–31.

Lyubashenko, Igor (2014), 'Euromaidan: from the students' protest to mass uprising,' in Bachmann, Klaus, Lyubashenko, Igor, *The Maidan uprising, separatism and foreign intervention. Ukraine's complex transition*, Peter Lang Edition, Frankfurt am Main, pp. 61–87.

Malfliet, Katlijn and Partmentier, Stephan (2010) *Russia and the Council of Europe. 10 years after*, Palgrave Macmillan.

Mandelson, Peter (2007), 'Russia and the EU', EU-Russia Centre, Brussels, 17 October 2007, SPEECH/07/629, in Marc, Leonard and Popescu, Nicu 'A power audit of EU-Russia relations', European Council of Foreign Relations, November 2007.

Mankoff, Jeffrey (2009), *Russian foreign policy. The return of the Great Power politics*, Rowman&Littlefield Publishers, INC, New York.

Manners, I. (2002), 'Normative Power Europe: A Contradiction in Terms?', *Journal of Common Market Studies*, No. 40, pp. 235–58.

Martinsen, Kaare Dahl (2002), „The Russian-Belarusian Union and the Near Abroad', Norwegian Institute for Defence Studies, Oslo.

Mearsheimer, John (1993), 'Back to the future: instability in Europe after the Cold War' in Lynn-Jones, S. (ed.) *The Cold War and after: prospects for peace*, Cmabridge MA: MIT Press, pp. 141–192.

Mearsheimer, John (1994/95), 'The false promise of international institutions', *International Security*, Vol. 19, Issue 3, pp. 5–49.

Medvedev, Sergei (2008), 'The stalemate in EU-Russia relations', in Hopf, Ted (ed.), *Russia's European choice*, Palgrave Macmillan.

Meister, Stefan (2010) 'The economization of Russian foreign policy', September, No. 10, *DGAP Standpunkt*.

Mid.ru (2012), 'Заявление официального представителя МИД России А.К.Лукашевича в связи с объявлением Грузией безвизового режима для граждан России' [Statement of A.K. Lukashevich, Official Representative of Russian Foreign Ministry, Concerning Georgia's Announcement of Visa-Free Regime for Russian Citizens], 2 March, available online at: http://en.mid.ru/en/web/guest/foreig n_policy/news/-/asset_publisher/cKNonkJE02Bw/content/id/16 6690?p_p_id=101_INSTANCE_cKNonkJE02BwHYPERLINK http:/ /en.mid.ru/en/web/guest/foreign_policy/news/-/asset_publishe r/cKNonkJE02Bw/content/id/166690?p_p_id=101_INSTANCE_cK NonkJE02Bw&_101_INSTANCE_cKNonkJE02Bw_languageId=ru_ RU"&HYPERLINK http://en.mid.ru/en/web/guest/foreign_poli cy/news/-/asset_publisher/cKNonkJE02Bw/content/id/166690?p _p_id=101_INSTANCE_cKNonkJE02Bw&_101_INSTANCE_cKNon kJE02Bw_languageId=ru_RU"_101_INSTANCE_cKNonkJE02Bw_la nguageId=ru_RU.

Milner, Helen (1992), 'International theories of cooperation among nations: strengths and weaknesses by Joseph Grieco', Review, *World Politics*, Vol. 44, no. 3, pp. 466–496.

Morgenthau, Hans (1965), *Politics among nations*, New York, Knopf.

Nappini, Floriana (2005), 'Partnership — principle and practice', European Summer Academy, Ohrid.

news.bigmir.net (2013), 'Янукович на саммите в Вильнюсе: Я 3,5 года один' [Yanukovych at the summit in Vilnius: For 3.5 years I am alone], 29 November, available online at: http://news.bigmir.ne t/ukraine/777872-Janukovich-na-sammite-v-Vil-njuse--Ja-3-5-goda-odin--VIDEO-.

Nye, Joseph S. Jr. (1993), *Understanding International Conflicts*, New York, Harper Collins.

Nygren, Bertil (2008), *The rebuilding of Greater Russia. Putin's foreign policy towards the CIS countries*, Routledge.

Nygren, Bertil (2009), 'Normative and ideological frictions between Russia and Europe: issues of security, economic integration, democracy and human rights', in Kanet, Roger E. (ed.), *A Resurgent Russia and the West: the European Union, NATO and beyond*, Dordrecht.

Ochmann, Cornelius (2009), 'EU Eastern Partnership: fine, but what about Russia?', *Spotlight Europe*, June, available online at: www.bertelsma nnstiftung.de/spotlight.

Oldberg, Ingmar (2007), 'Russia's great power ambitions and policy under Putin', in Kanet, Roger E., *Russia – re-emerging Great Power*, Palgrave Macmillan, pp. 13–31.

Oliker, Olga; Crane, Keith; Schwartz, Lowell H.; Yusupov, Catherine (2009), *Russian foreign policy. Sources and implications*, RAND Project Air Forces.

Orlov, Dmitri (2006), 'Политическая доктрина суверенной демократии' [The political doctrine of sovereign democracy], in Izvestiya, 30 November, available online at: http://izvestia.ru /news/319474, accessed 13 January 2016.

Pannier Bruce (2011), 'Azerbaijan supply agreement pumps new life into EU's energy plans', *Radio Free Europe*, January 13, available online at: http://www.rferl.org.

Parmentier, Florent (2008), 'The reception of EU neighbourhood policy', in Zaki, Laidi (ed.), *EU foreign policy in a globalized world*, Routledge, pp. 103–117.

Paszyc, Ewa (2010), 'Nord and South Stream won't save Gazprom', *OSW Commentary*, issue 35.

Pinder, John and Shishkov, Yuri (2002) *The EU & Russia. The promise of Partnership*, The Federal Trust of Education and Research, London.

Polish-Russian Group of Difficult Matters (2011), 'Rethinking EU-Russia relationship', interim report, The Center for Polish-Russian Dialogue and Understanding, Brussels, November.

Portela, C. (2007), 'Community policies with a security agenda: the worldview of Benita Ferrero-Waldner', *EUI Working papers*. RSCAS 2007/10, available online at: cadmus.iue.it/dspace/handle/181 4/6752.

Portnov, Andriy, Portnov, Tetiana (2015), 'The Ukrainian 'Eurorevolution': dynamics and meaning', in Viktor Stepanenko & Yaroslav Pylynskyi (eds.), *Ukraine after the Euromaidan. Challenges and hopes*, Peter Lang, Bern, Berlin, Bruxelles, Frankfurt am Main, New York, Oxford, Wien, pp. 59–73.

President of Russia (2009), 'News conference following Russia-EU summit', May 22, available online at: http://archive.kremlin.ru/eng /speeches/2009/05/22/1419_type82915_216713.shtml.

Putin Vladimir (2011), 'Новый интеграционный проект для Евразии — будущее, которое рождается сегодня' [New integration project for Eurasia — a future that is born today], in Izvestia, October 3, available online at: http://izvestia.ru/news/502761.

Putin, Vladimir (1999) 'Rossiia na rubezhe tysjachiletii' [Russia at the turn of the millennium], *Nezavisimaya Gazeta*, December 30, available online at: http://www.ng.ru/politics/1999-12-30/4_millenium.ht ml

Putin, Vladimir (2007a), '50 years of the European integration and Russia', March 25, available online at: http://www.belgium.mid.ru/press/1 18_en.html.

Putin, Vladimir (2007b) Speech at Munich Security Conference, 10 February, available online at: http://wn.com/Munich_Conference_on_Se-curity_Policy

Putin, Vladimir (2010), 'From Lisbon to Vladivostok', *Der Spiegel*, November 25, available online at http://www.spiegel.de/international/europe/from-lisbon-to-vladivostok-putin-envisions-a-russia-eu-free-trade-zone-a-731109.html.

Putin, Vladimir (2014a), Address by President of the Russian Federation, March 18, available online at: http://eng.kremlin.ru/news/6889.

Putin, Vladimir (2014b), Direct Line with Vladimir Putin, transcript, 17 April, available online at: http://en.kremlin.ru/events/president /news/page/101.

Putin, Vladimir (2014c), Conference of Russian ambassadors and permanent representatives, 1 July, available online at: http://en.kremlin.ru/events/president/news/46131.

Putin, Vladimir (2015a), 'Большая пресс-конференция Владимира Путина' [Vladimir Putin's annual press conference], 17 December, available online at: http://kremlin.ru/events/president/news/50 971.

Putin, Vladimir (2015b), Interview for the documentary 'Миропорядок' [The World Order], available online at: https://www.youtube.co m/watch?v=ZNhYzYUo42g.

Radio Free Europe Radio Liberty (2014), 'Russian Official Warns Moldova Over EU Association', 12 May, available online at: http://www.rferl.org/content/russian-official-warns-moldova-over-eu-assocoation /25381405.html.

Rettman, Andrew (2011), 'Russian president: EU's Parliament means nothing', *The EuObserver*, December 15, available online at: http://euobserver.com/24/114655.

Reuters (2012), 'Putin attacks EU sanctions on Belarus visit,' 31 May, available online at: http://www.reuters.com/article/us-russia-putin-belarus-idUSBRE84U1J220120601.

Reuters (2013), 'Russia-Ukraine talks fuel suspicion, anger in Kiev,' 7 December, available online at: http://www.reuters.com/article/us-russia-ukraine-idUSBRE9B606020131207#1bZi2F4EhRxLfCR2.97.

Reuters (2014), 'How the separatists delivered Crimea to Moscow', 13 March, available online at: http://in.reuters.com/article/2014/ 03/13/ukraine-crisis-russia-aksyonov-idINL6N0M93AH20140313.

Reuters (2016), 'Sanctions impact on Russia to be longer term, U.S. says', 12 January, available online at: http://www.reuters.com/article/us-ukraine-crisis-sanctions-idUSKCN0UQ1ML20160112.

Romaniuk, Scott Nicholas (2009), 'Rethinking EU-Russia relations: 'modern' cooperation or 'post modern' strategic partnership', *CEJISS*, issue 2.

Romanova, Tatiana (2010), 'The theory and practice of reciprocity in EU-Russia reltions', in Engelbrekt, Kjell and Nygren, Bertil (eds.), *Russia and Europe. Building bridges, digging trenches*, Routledge, pp. 60–81.

Rosefielde, Steven and Hlouskova, Romana (2007) 'Why Russia is Not a Democracy', *Comparative Strategy*, 26:3, pp. 215–229.

Rotaru, Vasile (2014), The Eastern Partnership. A turning point in EU-Russia relations? Military Publishing House, Bucharest.

RT (2014a), 'Crimea declares independence, seeks UN recognition,' 17 March, available online at: https://www.rt.com/news/crimea-refe rendum-results-official-250/.

RT (2014b), '10 more questions Russian military pose to Ukraine, US over MH17 crash,' 21 July, available online at: https://www.rt.com/new s/174496-malaysia-crash-russia-questions/.

Rukhadze, Vasili (2015), 'In the Face of Recent Russian-Abkhaz Disagreements, is Georgian-Abkhaz Dialogue Possible?' Eurasia Daily Monitor Volume: 12 Issue: 128, 9 July.

Rumer Eugene B. (2007), 'Chapter One: A Foreign Policy in Transition', *The Adelphi Papers*, Vol. 47, Issue 390, pp. 13–21.

Rumer, Eugene B. (2007), 'Chapter Two: Putin's Foreign Policy – A Matter of Interest', *The Adelphi Papers*, Vol. 47, Issue 390, pp. 23–42.

Russia Beyond the Headlines (2014), 'Report: Euphoria over 'return' of Crimea has passed among Russians', 30 March, available online at: http://rbth.com/society/2015/03/30/report_euphoria_over_retur n_of_crimea_has_passed_among_russians_44857.html.

Sakwa, Richard (2008), '''New Cold War' or twenty years' crisis? Russia and international politics', *International Affairs (Royal Institute of International Affairs 1944-)*, Vol. 84, No. 2: 241–267.

Sakwa, Richard (2011), 'Russia's Identity: Between the 'Domestic' and the 'International'', *Europe-Asia Studies*, Vol. 63, Issue 6, pp. 957–975.

Sakwa, Richard (2012), 'Sovereignty and democracy: constructions and contradictions in Russia and beyond', in Region: Regional Studies of Russia, Eastern Europe, and Central Asia, Volume 1, Number 1, pp. 3–27.

Sakwa, Richard (2015), *Frontline Ukraine. Crisis in the borderlands*, I.B. Tauris, London, New York.

Salvati, Federico (2015), 'Russia and Azerbaijan: a complicated relationship,' in Geopolitica, 15 March, available online at: http://www.ge opolitica.info/russia-and-azerbaijan/.

Schmitt, Carl (1996), *The concept of the political*, Chicago: University of Chicago press.

Secrieru, Stanislav (2014), 'How to Offset Russian Shadow Power? The Case of Moldova,' PISM Bulletin No. 125 (720), 31 October, pp. 1–2.

Selezneva, Ludmilla (2002), 'Post-Soviet Russian foreign policy: between doctrine and pragmatism', in European Security, 11:4, pp. 10–28.

Semenij, Olexij (2010), 'EU-Russia strategy and Eastern Partnership: Less Confrontation, More Cooperation?', Heinrich Boll Stiftung, September 16, available online at http://www.boell.de/internationalepolitik/europatransatlantik/europa-transatlantik-eu-russia-strategy-eastern-partnership-10113.html.

Shapovalova, Natalia (2014), 'The role of Crimea in Ukraine', in in Bachmann, Klaus, Lyubashenko, Igor, *The Maidan uprising, separatism and foreign intervention. Ukraine's complex transition*, Peter Lang Edition, Frankfurt am Main, pp. 227–267.

Shinoda, Hideaki (2000), *Re-examining Sovereignty. From Classical Theory to the Global Age*, Macmillan Press LTD, London.

Shoemaker, Wesley M. (2014), *Russia and The Commonwealth of Independent States*, Stryker-Post Publications, Lanham.

Sikorski, Radoslav (2009), 'The Eu's 'Eastern Partnership' is key to relations with Russia', *Europe's World*, summer, pp. 38–41.

Smith, Michael E. (2011), 'A liberal grand strategy in a realist world? Power, purpose and the EU's changing global role', *Journal of European Public Policy*, Vol. 18, Issue 2, pp. 144–163.

Solana, J. (2003), 'Une Europe sure dans un monde meillleur', available online at: http://ue.eu.int/ueDocs/cms_Data/docs/pressdata/FR/reports/76256.pdf.

Sputniknews (2013), 'Georgia Protests Putin's Visit to Abkhazia,' 26 August, available online at: http://sputniknews.com/russia/2013082 6/182977263/Georgia-Protests-Putins-Visit-to-Abkhazia.html.

Sputniknews (2015), 'Crimea—the way back home,' documentary film, available online at: http://sputniknews.com/russia/20150331/102 0271172.html.

Stepanenko, Viktor (2015), 'Ukraine's revolution as de-institutionalisation of the post-Soviet order,' in Viktor Stepanenko & Yaroslav Pylynskyi (eds.), *Ukraine after the Euromaidan. Challenges and hopes*, Peter Lang, Bern, Berlin, Bruxelles, Frankfurt am Main, New York, Oxford, Wien, pp. 29–47.

Strategiya Razvitii Otnoshenii Rossiiskoi Federatsii v Evropeiskim Soyuzom na Srednesrochnouyu Perspektivu (2000–2010 gg.), [The Medium-Term Strategy for development of Relations between the Russian Federation and the European Union (2000–2010)] (2000).

Stürmer, Michael (2011), *Putin & Noua Rusie*, ed. Litera, Chişinău.

Surkov, Vladislav (2006) 'Natsionalizatsiya budushchego', [The nationalization of the future], *Expert*, no. 43, 20 November, available online at: http://expert.ru/expert/2006/43/nacionalizaciya_buduschego/.

Surkov, Vladislav (2006), 'Национализация будущего' [The nationalization of the future], available online at: http://surkov.info/nacionalizaciya-budushhego-polnaya-versiya/.

Surkov, Vladislav (2008), 'Russian political culture: The view from utopia', Russian Social Science Review, 49(6), p. 81–97.

Surkov, Vladislav (2009), 'Nationalization of the future: paragraphs prosovereign democracy', Russian Studies in Philosophy, 47:4, pp. 8–21.

Sussex, Matthew (2012), 'Twenty years after the fall: continuity and change in Russian foreign and security policy', Global Change, Peace & Security: formerly Pacifica Review: Peace, Security & Global Change, Vol. 24, Issue 2, pp. 203–217.

Sutela, Pekka (2007), 'The economic future of Russia', International Journal of Economic Policy in Emerging Economies, vol. 1, pp. 21–33.

Swoboda, Hannes (2011), Interview given to the author in December.

Tass (2014), 'Russia freezes Lena bridge construction project till 2020', 24 November, available online at: http://tass.ru/en/russia/761460.

Taulus, Kim and Fratini, Piero Luigi (2010), 'EU-Russia energy relations', Euroconfidenciel.

Taylor, Paul (1999), 'The United Nations in the 1990s: Proactive Cosmopolitanism and the Issue of Sovereignty', Political Studies, vol. 47, no. 3.

Techau, Jan (2012), 'Russia's geopolitical Gazprom blunder', available online at http://carnegieeurope.eu/strategiceurope/?fa=49911.

The Atlantic (2014), 'A 24-Step Plan to Resolve the Ukraine Crisis', 26 August, available online at: http://www.theatlantic.com/international/archive/2014/08/a-24-step-plan-to-resolve-the-ukraine-crisis/379121/.

The Economist (2013), 'Why has Russia banned Moldovan wine?' 25 November, available online at: http://www.economist.com/blogs/economist-explains/2013/11/economist-explains-18.

The European Security Strategy (2003), available online at: http://www.consilium.europa.eu/uedocs/cmsUpload/78367.pdf.

The Guardian (2009), 'Embassy cables: Truth about Putin and Medvedev – over a bottle of vodka,' 19 March, available online at: http://www.theguardian.com/world/us-embassy-cables-documents/197735.

The Guardian (2013), 'Ukraine's EU trade deal will be catastrophic, says Russia,' 22 September, available online at: http://www.theguardian.com/world/2013/sep/22/ukraine-european-union-trade-russia.

The Guardian (2015), 'Georgia accuses Russia of violating international law over South Ossetia,' 14 July, available online at: http://www.the guardian.com/world/2015/jul/14/georgia-accuses-russia-of-violat ing-international-law-over-south-ossetia.

The Moscow Times (2015), 'Death of Novorossia: Why Kremlin Abandoned Ukraine Separatist Project,' 25 May, available online at: http://www.themoscowtimes.com/news/article/death-of-novoro ssia-why-kremlin-abandoned-ukraine-separatist-project/522320.ht ml.

The Telegraph (2014), 'I can take Kiev in two weeks, Vladimir Putin warns European leaders,' 1 September, available online at: http://www.tel egraph.co.uk/news/worldnews/europe/ukraine/11069070/I-can-t ake-Kiev-in-two-weeks-Vladimir-Putin-warns-European-leaders.ht ml.

The Treaty on European Union, available online at http://eur-lex.euro pa.eu/LexUriServ/LexUriServ.do?uri=OJ:C:2010:083:0013:0046:en:P DF.

Tichy, Lukas (2010), 'Energy security in the EU-Russia relations', Institute of International Relations, Prague.

Transparency International (2010), 'Corruption perception index 2010 results', available online at: http://www.transparency.org/policy_re search/surveys_indices/cpi/2010/results.

Trenin, Dmitri (2006), 'Russia leaves the West', *Foreign Affairs*, vol. 85, No. 4 (Jul.–Aug.), pp. 87–96.

Trenin, Dmitri (2007), 'Russia and Central Asia', in *Central Asia: Views from Washington, Moscow and Beijing*, Armonk, NY and London: ME Sharpe, pp. 75–137.

Trenin, Dmitri (2010a), 'Как менялась внешняя политика современной России, 1992–2010' [How did the Russian foreign policy change, 1992–2010], available online at: http://russia-2020.org/2010/10/0 6/russian-foreign-policy-perspective-2020/.

Trenin, Dmitri (2010b), 'Russia and Poland: a friendship that must not fail', December, available online at: http://www.cdi.org/russi a/johnson/russia-poland-friendship-dec-446.cfm

Trenin, Dmitri (2011), *Post-imperium: a Eurasian story*, Carnegie Endowment for International Peace, Washington, D.C.

Trenin, Dmitry (2005), 'Russia, the EU and the common neighbourhood', *Centre for European Reform*, available online at: http://www.cer.org.u k/publications/archive/essay/2005/russia-eu-and-common-neigh bourhood.

Tsygankov, Andrei P. (2006), *Russia's foreign policy. Change and continuity in national identity*, Rowman & Littlefield publishers INC.

Tumanov, Sergey; Gasparishvili, Alexander; Romanova, Ekaterina (2011), 'Russia–EU Relations, or How the Russians Really View the EU', *Journal of Communist Studies and Transition Politics*, 27:1, pp. 120–141.

Ukrainian Policy (2014), 'Strelkov declared Supreme Commander,' 12 May, available online at: http://ukrainianpolicy.com/donetsk-repu blic-coup-strelkov-girkin-now-supreme-commander/.

Ukrainskaya Pravda (2013), 'Азаров отказался от Соглашения об ассоциации с ЕС' [Azarov refused the Association Agreement with the EU], 21 November, available online at: http://www.pravd a.com.ua/rus/news/2013/11/21/7002657/.

Ukrinform.ua (2014), 'Явка виборців на псевдореферендумі в Криму була максимум 30–40 відсотків' [Turnout in psevdoreferendumi in Crimea would have been up 30–40 percent], 17 March, available online at: http://www.ukrinform.ua/rubric-politycs/1633549-yav ka_vibortsiv_na_psevdoreferendumi_v_krimu_bula_maksimum_30 _40_vidsotkiv___medglis_1918585.html.

Umland, Andreas (2011), 'EU and NATO policies on Eastern Europe: contradictory or complementary?', available online at: http://en.rian.r u/valdai_op/20110610/164548767.html.

Umland, Andreas (2016), 'Alexander Dugin and Moscow's New Right-Radical Intellectual Circles at the Start of Putin's Third Presidential Term 2012-2013: The Anti-Orange Committee, the Izborsk Club and the Florian Geyer Club in Their Political Context', *Europolity*, Vol. 2, No. 2, pp. 7-31.

Unian (2016), 'New Year with Ukraine-EU DCFTA', 4 January, available online at: http://www.unian.info/economics/1228645-new-year-w ith-ukraine-eu-dcfta.html.

Vahl, Marius (2007), 'EU-Russia relations in EU Neighbourhood Policies', in Malfliet, Katlijn; Verpoest, Lien and Vinokurov, Evgeny (eds.), *The CIS, the EU and Russia. The challenges of integration*, Palgrave Macmillan.

Verpoest, Lien (2007), 'Parallels and divergences in integration in Ukraine and Belarus', in Malfliet, Katlijn; Verpoest, Lien and Vinokurov, Evgeny (eds.), *The CIS, the EU and Russia. The challenges of integration*, Palgrave Macmillan.

Vzglyad (2015), 'За Крымом и Донбассом может последовать Закарпатье' [Transcarpathia might follow Crimea and Donbas], 29 June, available online at: http://vz.ru/world/2015/6/29/7534 01.html.

Waltz, Keneth N. (1979), *Theory of international politics*. New York: McGraw-Hill.

Webber, Mark (2000), Russia and Europe: conflict or cooperation? Macmillan Press LTD.

Whitman, R. (1998), *From Civilian Power to Superpower? The International Identity of the European Union*. London: Macmillan.

Whitman, Richard G. and Wolff, Stefan (2010), *The European Neighbourhood Policy in perspective*, Palgrave Macmillan.

Wiegand, Gunnar (2008), 'EU-Russian relations at a crossroads', *Irish Studies in International Affairs*, Vol. 19, pp. 9–15.

Wierbowska-Miazga, Agata (2011), 'The next stage of integration in the post-Soviet area', *East Week*, November 23, available online at: http://www.osw.waw.pl/en/publikacje/eastweek/2011.11-23/next-stage-integration-postsoviet-area.

Wilk, Andrzey (2014), 'Russian military intervention in Crimea', OSW Analyses, 5 March, available online at: http://www.osw.waw.pl/en/publikacje/analyses/2014-03-05/russian-military-intervention-crimea.

Wood, Steve (2011), 'Pragmatic power EUrope?', *Cooperation and Conflict*, 46, pp. 242–261.

Wydra, Doris and Puzl, Helga (2010), 'Democracy, security and energy: the Russian-EU relationship', SGIR 7th Pan-European International Relations Conference: September 9–11.

Yanukovych, Viktor (2014), Press conference in Rostov-on-Don, 28 February, available online at: https://www.youtube.com/watch?v=6NzaVCIQp_A.

Young, Oran R. (1989), International cooperation: building regimes for natural resources and the environment, Ithaca, NY, Cornell University Press.

Youngs, Richard (2010), The EU's role in world politics. A retreat from liberal internationalism, Routledge, Abingdon.

Yurgens, Igor (2010), 'The objectives and the price of modernization in Russia', *The EU-Russia center review*, Issue 15, October.

Zaki, Laidi (2008), 'European preferences and their reception', in Zaki, Laidi (ed.), *EU foreign policy in a globalized world*, Routledge, pp. 1–21.

Ziegler, Charles E. (2012), 'Conceptualizing sovereignty in Russian foreign policy: Realist and constructivist perspectives', International Politics Vol. 49, 4, 400–417.

Zimmermann, Hubert (2007), 'Realist Power Europe? The EU in the Negotiations about China's and Russia's WTO Accession', *Journal of Common Market Studies*, Vol. 45, Issue 4, pp. 813–832.

Zochowski, Piotr (2010), 'Russia's interest in the Mistral: the political and military aspects', *OSW Commentary*, issue 41.

Zubarevich, Natalia (2015), 'The Relations between the Center and the Regions', in Maria Lipman, Nikolay Petrov (eds.), *The state of Russia: what comes next?*, Palgrave Macmillan, New York, pp. 50–69.

ЛІГАБізнесІнформ (2014), 'Зачем Россия возобновляет торговую войну' [Why Russia is resuming the trade war], 29 Januay, available online at: http://biz.liga.net/all/all/stati/2699106-zachem-rossiya-vozobnovlyaet-torgovuyu-voynu.htm.

Путин, Владимир (2011), 'Новый интеграционный проект для Евразии — будущее, которое рождается сегодня' [Vladimir Putin, 'The new integrationist project for Eurasia—the future which is born today'], *Известия*, October 3, available online at: http://www.izvestia.ru/news/502761.

SOVIET AND POST-SOVIET POLITICS AND SOCIETY

Edited by Dr. Andreas Umland

ISSN 1614-3515

44   *Anastasija Grynenko in*
Zusammenarbeit mit Claudia Dathe
Die Terminologie des Gerichtswesens
der Ukraine und Deutschlands im
Vergleich
Eine übersetzungswissenschaftliche Analyse
juristischer Fachbegriffe im Deutschen,
Ukrainischen und Russischen
Mit einem Vorwort von Ulrich Hartmann
ISBN 3-89821-691-8

45   *Anton Burkov*
The Impact of the European
Convention on Human Rights on
Russian Law
Legislation and Application in 1996-2006
With a foreword by Françoise Hampson
ISBN 978-3-89821-639-5

46   *Stina Torjesen, Indra Overland (Eds.)*
International Election Observers in
Post-Soviet Azerbaijan
Geopolitical Pawns or Agents of Change?
ISBN 978-3-89821-743-9

47   *Taras Kuzio*
Ukraine – Crimea – Russia
Triangle of Conflict
ISBN 978-3-89821-761-3

48   *Claudia Šabić*
"Ich erinnere mich nicht, aber L'viv!"
Zur Funktion kultureller Faktoren für die
Institutionalisierung und Entwicklung einer
ukrainischen Region
Mit einem Vorwort von Melanie Tatur
ISBN 978-3-89821-752-1

49   *Marlies Bilz*
Tatarstan in der Transformation
Nationaler Diskurs und Politische Praxis
1988-1994
Mit einem Vorwort von Frank Golczewski
ISBN 978-3-89821-722-4

50   *Марлен Ларюэль (ред.)*
Современные интерпретации
русского национализма
ISBN 978-3-89821-795-8

51   *Sonja Schüler*
Die ethnische Dimension der Armut
Roma im postsozialistischen Rumänien
Mit einem Vorwort von Anton Sterbling
ISBN 978-3-89821-776-7

52   *Галина Кожевникова*
Радикальный национализм в России
и противодействие ему
Сборник докладов Центра «Сова» за 2004-
2007 гг.
С предисловием Александра Верховского
ISBN 978-3-89821-721-7

53   *Галина Кожевникова и Владимир*
Прибыловский
Российская власть в биографиях I
Высшие должностные лица РФ в 2004 г.
ISBN 978-3-89821-796-5

54   *Галина Кожевникова и Владимир*
Прибыловский
Российская власть в биографиях II
Члены Правительства РФ в 2004 г.
ISBN 978-3-89821-797-2

55   *Галина Кожевникова и Владимир*
Прибыловский
Российская власть в биографиях III
Руководители федеральных служб и
агентств РФ в 2004 г.
ISBN 978-3-89821-798-9

56   *Ileana Petroniu*
Privatisierung in
Transformationsökonomien
Determinanten der Restrukturierungs-
Bereitschaft am Beispiel Polens, Rumäniens
und der Ukraine
Mit einem Vorwort von Rainer W. Schäfer
ISBN 978-3-89821-790-3

57   *Christian Wipperfürth*
Russland und seine GUS-Nachbarn
Hintergründe, aktuelle Entwicklungen und
Konflikte in einer ressourcenreichen Region
ISBN 978-3-89821-801-6

58   *Togzhan Kassenova*
From Antagonism to Partnership
The Uneasy Path of the U.S.-Russian
Cooperative Threat Reduction
With a foreword by Christoph Bluth
ISBN 978-3-89821-707-1

59   *Alexander Höllwerth*
Das sakrale eurasische Imperium des
Aleksandr Dugin
Eine Diskursanalyse zum postsowjetischen
russischen Rechtsextremismus
Mit einem Vorwort von Dirk Uffelmann
ISBN 978-3-89821-813-9

ibidem-Verlag / *ibidem* Press
Melchiorstr. 15
70439 Stuttgart
Germany

ibidem@ibidem.eu
ibidem.eu